Initiation Ceremonies

An Advanced Study in Anthropology

Initiation

FRANK W. YOUNG

Cornell University

Ceremonies

A Cross-Cultural Study
of
Status Dramatization

THE BOBBS-MERRILL COMPANY, INC.
A Subsidiary of Howard W. Sams & Co., Inc.
Publishers · Indianapolis · New York · Kansas City

Ward H. Goodenough

CONSULTING EDITOR *University of Pennsylvania*

Acknowledgments

The introduction will perhaps make the reader sufficiently aware of my intellectual debts, but special acknowledgment is due John W. M. Whiting and G. P. Murdock. Both will probably continue to disagree heartily with my conclusions, but they have nevertheless supported the effort from the time they learned of it and have materially contributed to its completion. My direct contact with this line of thought came through the teaching of William W. Lambert. I consider it the great merit of his instruction that I was encouraged to consider alternatives, and I hope this study does not transgress his fundamental rule that it does not matter much what position one takes as long as one observes the rules of the game.

My wife has accepted with good humor a two-year delay in our cooperative work while I completed this study "that could easily be done in a summer." More significantly, she has helped out whenever technical or conceptual snarls began to get out of hand, which seemed to be most of the time.

Millicent R. Ayoub, Albert S. Anthony, Peter Hammond, Jules Henry, John Hitchcock, Lee Munroe, A. Kimball Romney, David Schneider, Leigh Triandis, and Arthur Tuden kindly supplied unpublished data or other information on which this research depended. Carolyn Bacdayan, Bernice Beagles, and Joan Brownell helped with the coding, which in this kind of study is an especially crucial operation. Beverly Andrews typed the manuscript.

This investigation was supported by two small grants (M 3740A and M 5625A) from the National Institute of Mental Health, and the completion of the manuscript was made possible by a grant-in-aid from the Social Science Research Council. I am indebted to these institutions and to the individuals who helped in the various ways mentioned above.

FRANK W. YOUNG
June 1964

Contents

Tables and Figures

Introduction

This book is a somewhat extended reaction to the work of John W. M. Whiting and his associates in the field of culture and personality studies. The original plan was to make a brief reinterpretation of a cross-cultural study of initiation ceremonies proposed by these investigators. But one thing led to another—from the study of male initiation ceremonies to that of female and then to a custom complex widely known as the couvade, which this study prefers to call parenthood initiation ceremonies. In the course of this work one could not avoid rethinking certain fundamental methodological issues in cross-cultural research, as well as alternative lines of theory.

Thus, the main theme of the book is an attempt to test the hypothesis that the degree of solidarity of a given social system determines the degree to which status transitions within it will be dramatized. Given such a starting point, it is necessary to show that the phenomena of initiation ceremonies may be interpreted adequately in terms of the dramatization dimension. Chapter 1 deals with this problem, as it applies both to male and female ceremonies. Then, in order to simplify the analysis, female and parenthood initiation are put aside until Chapter 6. It turns out that male solidarity operates in the context of the whole community, while female solidarity is limited by family structure. Thus, although the form of hypothesis remains the same, the empirical context changes. This shift of social unit permits a useful replication, but it also necessitates an analysis of the interrelations of family and community, which is the substance of Chapter 7.

The Sociogenic–Psychogenic Dialogue

However, all this discussion takes place in the shadow of Whiting's initial hypothesis and cross-cultural evidence. What develops is therefore a dialogue between two types of explanations of group-level phenomena like initiation ceremonies. The solidarity hypothesis, because it takes as causal the structure of the social meanings held by the group and interprets individual tendencies as operating within such structures and having no independent effect, is characterized as a sociogenic position. Whiting's hypothesis is labeled psychogenic because it begins with social structure—"primary institutions"—but asserts the independent causal efficacy of intervening modal personality tendencies in determining group-level phenomena—"secondary institutions" or "projective systems." Let it be said here, to be repeated later, that *both* explanations involve individual and group factors. What is at issue is the relative efficacy of the two classes of determinants for explaining *institutionalized* customs.

As it is pursued with the data of the Human Relations Area Files and a functionalist framework, the sociogenic-psychogenic dialogue involves many methodological problems. Because no fundamental understanding of these two types of explanation is possible without an analysis of their methodological underpinnings, considerable space throughout the book and the whole of Chapter 3 are given over to them. Chapter 8 returns to these problems. It is an old maxim that the manner in which one achieves a result is often more important than the result itself because only explicitly obtained findings can be legitimately admitted to the corpus of acceptable scientific knowledge. In the present case this rule is even more pressing. In cross-cultural work one cannot even be sure one has a result without an intensive probing of procedures.

Dramatization as Social Communication

The theory that guides this study is at least as old as Durkheim and was applied to ceremonies by Radcliffe-Brown.[1] But these two writers

---

[1] All bibliographic references in this book are presented in this manner. The complete citations appear under References, pp. 178-181.

are not explicit about the dynamics of the process of dramatizing social solidarity. It is at this point that the work of Erving Goffman and that of Kenneth Burke are helpful. In these new terms, both solidarity and dramatization are seen as human creations that must be constantly renewed and revised for various "audiences." Dramatization is the communication strategy typically employed by solidarity groups in order to maintain their highly organized, but all the more vulnerable, definition of the situation.

The relationship between the organization of social meanings and the dramatic communication of them is probably one of circular causality, even though the actual test of the hypothesis takes solidarity as the independent variable. This research does not take the more radical step—suggested by Burke—of considering the forms of social communication as the crucial determinants of sociological phenomena. It does, however, view such phenomena in formal terms and seek explanations in the interactions of individuals rather than in the inner dynamics of personality.

The Meaning of the Ceremony

This research, as has been stated, is concerned primarily with the functions of initiation ceremonies, and a functional explanation is proposed in Chapter 2 and tested in subsequent chapters. But the problem of the social meaning of initiation is always in the background. Unfortunately, this problem is embedded in a tangle of issues that are not easily resolved. The very definitions of function and meaning are clouded. The usual distinctions make function an objective relationship between the rite and the social system to which it relates, while meaning is the cluster of culturally ordered ideas by which it is summarized.

But some writers do not separate meaning from function, and others would argue that meaning can be objective. Other dimensions of the problem include the use of verbal—myth—versus behavioral—ritual—data as a basis of interpreting the symbols; an emphasis on a part of the ritual, such as circumcision, versus the whole, as in Van Gennep's processual concept; and the weight to be placed on the native's particular interpretation relative to one that allows cross-cultural comparison. A review of the work of a number of investigators who have attacked these problems illustrates the issues and clarifies the strategy adopted here. Despite the criticisms made of previous attempts, the present handling of the meaning problem accepts the main trend of this work.

Concern with a part of the ritual characterizes the interpretations of Bettelheim (1954) and Eliade (1958), but they differ in their reliance on native interpretation. For Bettelheim, the meaning of "symbolic wounds" such as subincision is that men can be like women in some respects. The similarity that he finds is in the attempt on the part of men to make their genital organs like those of women. Bettelheim does not reject native testimony, but the recondite character of his interpretation, turning as it does on male envy of the procreative functions of women, is not the sort of thing that a native—or anybody else for that matter—normally brings up in conversation. Eliade's interpretation makes much of the native conception of initiation as death and rebirth. This concept, found in certain societies only, he takes to be the central meaning of the rite. He is interested in relating the native view to Christian thinking about baptism.

What can be said at this point as to the validity of these interpretations of the meaning of initiation? The pilot study that preceded the main effort of this research included various native beliefs and practices relevant to these interpretations. The finding was that subincision, tooth extraction, clitoridectomy, and belief in death and rebirth are so infrequent (one or two cases in a sample of 54 communities) as to be unresearchable on a comparative basis. So whatever the truth of these two interpretations, they do not apply to the majority of societies.

As for the truth of the interpretations in the few cases to which they do apply, we have only the word of Bettelheim and Eliade that they are valid. The scanty and overinterpreted case material they offer as evidence is unacceptable. One is reminded of Van Gennep's (1960:72-73) comment on circumcision: "for the sake of sensible interpretation it is really regrettable that the Jews should have practiced it. . . . if the Jews had linked themselves to Yahweh by perforating the septum, how much fewer would have been the errors in ethnographic literature."

The interpretations of Van Gennep (1960) and Whiting, Kluckhohn, and Anthony (1958:359-70), Burton and Whiting (1961:85-95), who respectively hypothesize the meaning to be "social transition" and what may be labeled "giving up one identification for another," are much more adequate in terms of their capacity to make sense out of the whole initiation ceremony. Both writers support their interpretations with comparative data, although the emphasis, of necessity, is on behavioral facts and observable customs.

Van Gennep proposed (1960:1-13), in one of the lasting contributions of the naturalistic tradition in anthropology, that the initiation ceremony conveys three submeanings—separation, transition, and incorporation—all of which may be summarized as social transition. He claimed that this scheme covers all rites of passage, but he admitted that the "three subcategories are not developed to the same extent by all peoples or in every ceremonial pattern" (1960:11). His hypothesis is restricted by the content of the ceremonies—he must find particular kinds of ritual content in order to judge initiation rites to be present. A further weakness is that one or another of his three phases is sometimes entirely absent; incorporation, for example, is not an invariable component of the ceremony, as will be shown in Chapter 1. But even more serious is the omission of many customs that are a functional part of the ceremonies. Furthermore, the rules for interpreting particular customs as reflecting one of the three phases are not given. For instance, does hazing reflect separation, transition, or incorporation?

Whiting's hypothesis seems inadequate in these respects too. Any one of four categories of custom may indicate an initiation ceremony. These are "separation from women," "tests of fortitude," "genital operations," and "hazing." This definition does cover most of the elaborate dramatizations, but what about simple festive attention? Moreover, we may doubt that the first pair of customs communicates the meaning of giving up a female identification or that the second pair means accepting adult men as a reference group. Admittedly, Whiting believes that the meaning of the ritual stimulates unconscious mental processes in the boy. But this assumption does not resolve a basic problem: How can a researcher be sure that a given custom will activate these unconscious processes?

Now each of these interpretations involves a complex methodology for arriving at the general meaning of the rite. First, particular customs are assigned particular, tentative meanings. Van Gennep takes seclusion practices, for example, to reflect removal from the nonsexual world, and Whiting interprets them as isolation from women. With other customs the assigned meaning may be more formal, as when Van Gennep says that circumcision is "nothing more than a rite of sexual differentiation on the same order as the first (ritual) assigning of dress, instruments, or tools proper to each sex" (1960:72). Then the specific meanings are collected and shown to converge on a general meaning, such as social transition or assumption of a new identity. The hypothesis as to the meaning of the rite is tested indirectly when the more general functional hypothesis is studied comparatively. Van Gennep compares across cultures and across different types of rites of passage. Whiting's cross-cultural study, which will be analyzed in detail in Chapter 4, is more rigorous.

Criteria for Interpreting the Meaning of the Ceremony

The meaning assigned to initiation ceremonies depends very much on the methodological rules that are adopted. The essential feature of the methodology of the present study is that a successful test of the general hypothesis is taken as validation of the meanings assigned to particular customs. If the submeanings are encompassed by the general meaning, the procedure is quite satisfactory. This indirect route is necessary because there are so many possibilities for interpreting the meaning of particular items that are not open to test. Even in this brief discussion, for instance, circumcision has been hypothesized by various writers to mean "envy of female genitals," "sign of male authority and identification object," and "indicator of sex differentiation." And these hardly tap the variety that the natives themselves might suggest.

This procedure assumes that a ritual can be assigned a meaning that is general enough to apply across cultures. It does not deal with the many special interpretations that a questionnaire or a projective test might reveal in particular cultures. These must be excluded from comparative studies unless they can be shown to be submeanings of an interpretation that is cross-culturally feasible. However, it seems necessary to add another criterion to the above procedure: The hypothesized meaning must be applicable to all instances of the phenomena. After all, a concept like "inhibitor of potentially disruptive emotions" might be cross-culturally valid without being relevant to a wide range of customs that are typically part of initiation ceremonies.

But how do we recognize a legitimate instance of initiation? That is the function of a concept and its empirical indicators, but the different theories referred to above suggest different concepts that intentionally omit certain aspects of the data. Such conceptual relativity does not excuse the omission of instances that, in the terms of a given concept, should have been covered. It is this deficiency that is the crux of the present criticism of the concepts of Whiting and Van Gennep. If initiations are instances of social transition rituals, then they should manifest the three types of customs assigned to such ceremonies. Similarly, if the ritual is a mechanism of reidentification, it should contain all the cogs required.

Meaning and the Dramatization Concept

What is the effect of applying these criteria to the dramatization concept? The interpretation of meaning that it suggests is that the ritual conveys distinction, importance, or special status. According to the rules stated above, (1) all the submeanings assigned to particular customs should be consistent with this general meaning; and (2) the general meaning should apply to the whole range of items that reflect dramatization.

On the first point let us turn to some well-known commentators. With respect to the genital operation of circumcision, Firth says:

> Its real meaning is usually to confer the appropriate material token of distinction upon the individual who has been the subject of the qualifying ritual. Among primitive nonliterate peoples for whom a written diploma is an impossibility, an unalterable bodily mark, a pattern of scars, a mutilation, of a kind which no person is likely to attempt to perform on himself, is an excellent means of classification [1936:465].

Thus, if genital operations are simply assigned the general meaning of distinction, importance, and so on, particular acts and symbols may be interpreted adequately.

Radcliffe-Brown indicates how the same meaning may be assigned to more unusual customs:

> In the Andamans the name of a dead person is avoided from the occurrence of the death to the conclusion of mourning; the name of a person mourning for a dead relative is not used; there is avoidance of the name of a youth or girl who is passing through the ceremonies that take place at adolescence; a bride or bridegroom is not spoken of or to by his or her own name for a short time after the marriage. For the Andamanese the personal name is a symbol of the social personality, i.e., of the position that an individual occupies in the social structure and the social life. The avoidance of a personal name is symbolic recognition of the fact that at the time the person is not occupying a normal position in the social life. It may be added that a person whose name is thus temporarily out of use is regarded as having for the time an abnormal ritual status [1956:146-47].

But what about hazing or beatings? How can such painful treatment be interpreted as conferring distinction? We are reminded of a passage in one of Ralph Linton's books:

> There was an old English custom, called "beating the bounds" in which a villager would take the boys once a year around the bounds of the village territory and at each point marker give the boys a thrashing so that the boundaries would be impressed on their memories, enabling them later on to recall clearly the limits of the territory. Also, when a boy's father introduced him to someone important, he would knock him down at the important man's feet, saying, "Now, you'll remember this." [1956:38].

At this point one is prompted to object that "ritual importance" is such a broad meaning that it cannot help but apply to all dramatic customs of sex-role recognition. While this is true, and underlines the adequacy of the interpretation for handling the variety of customs, it is not necessarily a criticism. If "ritual distinction" turns out to be sterile and incapable of articulation with a heuristic theory, then it is too thin. The evidence of the rest of the book will help to decide this point. But it should be noted that other investigators would probably not deny ritual distinction as a meaning of the initiation ceremony. It is simply that they would go further in specifying other meanings for which there is inadequate justification.

1. *The Social Recognition of Sex Role*

> The fundamental business of growing up is accomplished every-where; and although methods and forms of behavior vary tremen-dously in different primitive cultures, they are usually dramatic. Whether in puberty rites or their educational equivalents, the over-whelming purpose of this dramatization is to emphasize and impress beyond the shadow of a doubt that childhood and all its parts have been left behind; to make sure that the individual has received communion with the deepest cultural ideals; and to announce and stress that henceforth he is an adult, responsible for his own acts and for his own share of group responsibilities [Charles 1946:261].

If society did not depend upon social communication, the cere-monies surrounding puberty, parenthood, marriage, and death might not exist. But men cannot rely upon their physical nature for the organization of society, and cultural ways of dividing people into categories and impressing them with their jobs have developed. Some of these patterns of social communication concern the cyclical events of group life—the birth of a culture hero or the harvesting of crops—and have been called "rites of intensification." Other rituals relate to the changes in the status of individuals as they move from one sector of the social structure to another. These have been called the "rites of passage." Since individuals do not go through life all at the same pace, the ceremonies that mark these transitions are not cyclical, although they are periodic. However, in most societies there is a tendency for ceremonies to cluster, either because candidates for one type of ceremony converge on a particular time, as with June

9

weddings, or because two ceremonies are combined, as with the blending of girls' puberty rites and the new year ceremony among the Yurok Indians of California.

Because they seem to differ so sharply from ceremonies in industrial society, the rites of passage of primitive peoples—and initiation ceremonies in particular—have always excited a great interest among social scientists and nonspecialists alike. Partial equivalents like the bar mizvah and the coming out of debutantes are confined to parts of modern populations only. Also, they do not involve the elaboration that occurs in some primitive groups; there are exceptions, like the practices of German dueling socities, but in general the ceremonies of modern groups are more restrained. It is generally unrecognized, on the other hand, that in addition to their striking aspects, primitive initiation ceremonies have an equal range of more obviously social gestures, such as the presentation of gifts, assumption of a new name or of adult clothing, festive attention in one form or another, or special performances.

What distinguishes the adolescent ceremonies of primitive and modern is not so much the range of practices, but the level of abstraction of the symbolism. Modern society is more concerned with general symbolic ideas. Confirmation in a religious group comes after a training period in dogma, symbols, and practices, and the ritual itself depends upon general, rather than concrete, symbolism. Perhaps a relationship exists between the heterogeneity of the candidates and the universalism of the symbols. Modern religions, dealing with millions of young people of diverse cultural backgrounds, must develop ways of transcending such diversity. In contrast, a small native community can recall the connotations of a particular tattoo despite its lack of association with a wider range of ideas. The rather concrete ritual practices of fraternities are not an exception to this hypothesis. While their membership is often small and homogeneous like that of a primitive group, even so, most clubs and student associations must appeal to general ideas of fraternal fellowship.

Although a test of the foregoing hypothesis is not the object here, the evidence to be reviewed will go far to confirm it. Its mention calls attention to a common characteristic of both primitive and modern initiation ceremonies: their dramatic quality. The ritual acts and their setting evoke ideas and emotions, and sometimes action, in a relatively passive audience. Dramatic communication achieves its effect by proposing new combinations of stimuli, which, however, call up and quicken old memories. The sight of a boy stoically undergoing circumcision or being beaten with thorns or enduring the stings of ants is an extremely dramatic event. And it is remembered.

Even the absence of a person is dramatic; it is remarkable, especially in face-to-face communities, when a person is not present. Why is it bad luck for the groom to see the bride in her white wedding dress before the ceremony begins? Because it ruins the effect of her entrance, erodes the sharpness of her image, and reflects, very likely, a lack of cooperation and social sensitivity among the performers that eventually leads to difficulties that others label bad luck. Of course, certain preparations can heighten the effect still more. Fasting, isolation, adornment, physical pain, and drugs are well-known ways by which primitives and moderns seek to participate more intensely in dramatic communication.

No one denies the dramatic side of initiation ceremonies, and theorists from Durkheim to Goffman have stressed its importance, but the implications have not been developed or systematically tested. One is led initially to a definition of initiation rites as the more dramatic forms of sex-role recognition. The various components of the ceremonies may be interpreted as the more striking ways by which some societies call attention to the shift in a young person's status from youth to a functional member of his sex. All societies must give social recognition to the differences between age levels and the sexes, but different kinds of social structure require more or less sharp distinctions. Dramatization is a way of underlining these primary social classifications, and finding the reason for which some societies do this more than others is the basic problem of this research.

An Operational Definition of Initiation Ceremonies

Modern anthropology attacks a problem like initiation ceremonies by drawing a sample of the ethnographic accounts of societies from all parts of the world and from different historical periods and then extracting the relevant data. Anthropologists are in general agreement as to what they mean by initiation ceremonies and usually report them if they occur in the tribe under study. But for the comparative purposes of this research, it was necessary to formulate more specific rules for defining the pool of relevant customs.

A pilot study indicated the utility of the following three criteria: (a) The custom must occur periodically in the same general form and be supervised at least in part by the adults of the society; (b) it must apply to all adolescents of one sex only; and (c) of a series of initiation events extending over a period of years, only the most elaborate is to be considered.

The first criterion excluded customs that occur sporadically, such as the hazing of Chiricahua Apache warrior novices when they are out on raids. This rule also excluded the casual personal decorations like tooth-blackening or tattooing that young people acquire by themselves or with the help of wandering specialists.

The second criterion excluded customs like marriages and funerals that usually apply in the same form to both sexes or to male and female at the same time; it excluded also a very few cases of initiation ceremonies, those conducted for both sexes. The other requirement of the second rule, that the candidates be young people, excluded practices like infantile male circumcision or the resubincision often practiced by older Australian aborigines. In only a few cases were such divergent customs not rejected by the application of the first or third rules, but even these few would have introduced extraneous data.

The third criterion helped to select for analysis one of a series of rituals that may continue throughout a man's life. Like the Masons, some Australian tribes have a sequence of degrees through which they must pass. The pilot investigation showed, however, that the most elaborate ceremony served the purposes of this study best. It should be added that when two ceremonial events, say, a feast and scarification, were separated by only a few months but were functionally a part of the pattern of social recognition given to individuals in that society, the two events were considered a unit.

Underlying all three criteria is a conception of a ritual event. Since Durkheim, anthropologists have distinguished the everyday secular customs from those that are discontinuous, extraordinary, or emotionally charged. An example is the consumption of particular foods that on certain occasions may not be eaten or must be eaten in a special manner. Basically, the distinction between the secular and the sacred rests on the difference in the native's attitude toward the custom, but in practice his behavior or special artifacts, such as ceremonial dress, are clear indicators.

In retrospect, the chief deficiency of the criteria is that they include that of age. Perhaps a stricter application of the other rules, particularly the third, and more attention to only the ritualized, out-of-the-ordinary events might have made the age specification unnecessary. Then one would have defining criteria that are purely social, and so eliminate a built-in association of this type of ceremony with physical age. But in practice it is difficult to avoid "adolescent" ceremonies. The fact is that a strong association exists between age and the dramatic recognition of sex role. Despite Van Gennep's (1960:65ff.) demonstration that this is not always so—by citing the occasional instances when married women or old men undergo initiation along with adolescents—it is still typically so.

The pilot study indicated, furthermore, that is is not always possible to use age at initiation as a criterion. In most cases it was reported, quite imprecisely for purposes of quantification, as "around puberty." Actually, this phrase is quite accurate. What happens in native practice is that the elders wait several years until a number of boys are "ready." Thus, some boys may be quite a bit older while some may be as young as seven or eight; the latter are usually more mature or are the sons of important men.

What Van Gennep should have emphasized, but did not, is that initiation does not confer the status of responsible adult. When one reads the ethnographic reports closely, it is clear that even initiated youths are still under close supervision. They may not be permitted to marry, or if they do, the couple lives in the parental domestic establishment. A young man may still have to wait some years before he is allowed to go on raids or speak freely in councils. The frequent practice of allowing initiated boys a great deal of sexual freedom after their ceremony is interpreted more accurately as an allowance for youthful experimentation than as an attitude of responsible adulthood. By and large native youth are capable of being accepted as responsible adults, and are so accepted, at about the age of 18; this is quite comparable to the practice in industrialized countries.

Another problematic application of these three criteria appears in connection with the Orokaiva of New Guinea. This tribe has a ceremony for boys and girls together and was therefore excluded from the study under the second rule. In general, the rule also excluded the bisexual "initiation" ceremonies of children, as among the Hopi and Navaho, and such modern specializations as high school graduation. It was not applied so rigorously in the study as to eliminate the Timbira or Mandan, where one or two girls seem to be more a part of the setting—like a mascot or showpiece—than regular initiates. The Orokaiva were the only group out of about a hundred that have initiation ceremonies which are similar in other respects to the modal pattern but which apply to both sexes—there is a suspicion of missionary influence that might explain its deviant status. In the main, initiation ceremonies of the type studied here are held exclusively for one sex.

Even when delimited according to these criteria, the range of items that qualify as ways of dramatizing the sex role is very wide. For comparative purposes many items in the study were grouped. Subincision, superincision, and circumcision, for example, were classified more grossly as "genital operations"; otherwise there would have been insufficient instances for analysis.

A Measure of Sex-Role Dramatization

In addition to apparent content similarity, the formal dimension underlying the diversity of customs was used as a basis for grouping items. This content-free, formal dimension was arrived at through the use of Guttman scaling, the procedures of which dictated further combination of items. The details, and the deficiencies, of the present use of this scaling technique are given in Chapter 3, but the essence of it is the arrangement of social attributes into unidimensional cumulative sequences from which degrees of dramatization emerge.

Table 1 shows the scale that was developed for measuring degrees of sex-role dramatization.

Of the 54 societies in the study sample (Chapter 3 describes the sample characteristics), 60 per cent had no dramatic forms of sex-role recognition for males, and 42 per cent had none for females. Many of these communities did have formal education, or they required a boy to move out of the domestic establishment at adolescence, but these practices do not meet the criteria of dramatization listed above. In

TABLE 1. **Scale of Dramatic Sex-Role Recognition for Males and Females**

Step number	Item content	Percentage of sample communities	
		Male recognition	*Female recognition*
0	Undramatic recognition only (following items not present)	60*	43
1	Customary minimal social recognition (gift, party, change of name, etc.)	7	20
2	Personal dramatization (initiate is ceremonially dressed or adorned)	15	16
3	Organized social response (group dresses up and/or performs)	9	17
4	Affective social response (beating or severe hazing of initiates)	9	4
	Total cases = 100 per cent	(54)	(54)
	Percentage with initiation ceremonies (steps 1-4)	40	57

* All numbers not in parentheses are percentages.

a few cultures, like the Koryak, young people simply grow up and begin working as adults. Thus, initiation ceremonies proper begin with step 1 and constitute 40 and 57 per cent of the sample for males and females respectively. If the presence of a custom at the level of step 1 or above is taken as indicating dramatic sex-role recognition, the table shows that these are more prevalent for girls than for boys.

The proportions for each step are given separately, but the steps are cumulative. This means that a society with step 3 of male dramatization also has all the other lower items. Because of this cumulative pattern, the table implicitly contains the information that 18 per cent of the sampled societies have as part of their ceremony some kind of organized social response to the initiate, as indicated in steps 3 and 4. It is assumed that if a society has some form of dramatic recognition, it still confers informal recognition, although such practices were not actually dealt with in the study (and are inadequately reported). Technically speaking, step 0 is a residual category. Nonetheless, the table allows us to conclude that male initiation rites are generally more elaborate or intense than those for females. This fact shows up when the proportions are compared for males and females at the level of minimal recognition (step 1) and again with respect to affective social response (step 4). It is even more pronounced when the percentages are recalculated for only those societies with some dramatic form of recognition.

The applicability of the same scale for both sexes suggests that a general process is operating. When the categories are arranged in this unidimensional pattern, the content of the items recedes in importance and the *degree of dramatization* emerges. The measure is not content-less, but it becomes content-free. Thus, the scaling technique combines with theory to bring out the formal dimension underlying the diversity of customs. The initial categorization on the basis of item content reduced the variety to a great extent, and the scaling procedure carried the process further.

Along with the degree of dramatization, the scale may be interpreted as reflecting increasing social preparation. The simplest way to call attention to a person is to make a social gesture. Such customs (step 1) make a claim on the community's stock of accepted symbols and result in consensual validation of a boy's or girl's new status. Thus, if it is the custom for children to go naked and a father gives his son a loin cloth, he is asking the community to agree with him about the maturity of the boy. The second step in the scale also applies to the initiate's person and requires only the amount of social preparation necessary for acquiring the costume or paint that is used for decoration.

Step 3, however, brings in the active participation of members of the audience. Their response may include not only the expenditure for any adornment but also sacrifice of time and energy necessary for practicing the song or stunt they present. The last step requires even more social preparation. Hazing or beating of initiates presupposes a complex consensus in the community regarding the means and results of such extreme measures. Otherwise, such a custom could get out of hand and a father might decide that his son's tormentors had exceeded their commission. Perhaps it is to avoid just such repercussions that parents are often excluded from the more intense aspects of the ceremony and those in charge of the initiates are responsible members of the community. Even so, the arousal of high affect among initiates and elders by physical means is a delicate social undertaking.

Other Attributes of the Ceremony

The attributes listed above—customary minimal social recognition, personal dramatization, organized social response, and affective social response—fit into a unidimensional cumulative sequence; that is to say, they scale. The dramatization dimension is thus shown to be a valid formal approach toward the interpretation of initiation ceremonies.

These four categories, however, did not exhaust the attributes of initiation ceremonies. There were several customs that did not scale but were still statistically associated with the measure. These illuminate the phenomenon of initiation in various ways.

The seclusion of the candidate has always been considered an integral part of rites of passage. Usually such seclusion is actual physical separation, in either a bush camp or a menstrual hut, although in a few cases the initiate may simply be socially segregated by the observance of avoidance taboos. There is in fact a strong association of seclusion with dramatization. For both sexes, it is characteristic of almost the full range of dramatization, though the association is stronger for males than for females.[1] Had it not reduced the efficiency of the measure, it might have been retained as a scale step, and in a larger sample it would probably add rather than detract. More thoroughgoing analysis may uncover the reason why seclusion is sometimes absent in dramatic sex-role recognition. It may be that this custom more often escapes the notice of ethnographers or that living arrangements make it unfeasible. Another possibility is that a functional alternative of "ritual visibility" substitutes for it, as when the naked pubescent girls of Ontong Java parade through the village.

Another category of cultural content that almost scales is "ritual restrictions and requirements," that is, all the unusual observances

[1] For males this item overlaps with personal adornment, step 2, with only one error. In the female scale it cuts off about half of step 1, but with three errors. (See Chapter 3 for a discussion of scale errors.)

expected of the initiate. These include restrictions on speaking, looking at people, touching, scratching, eating, moving, sexual relations, etc. The rectilinear eating customs of West Point plebes are a modern instance.

In some cases an initiate may be required to perform a daily ritual cleansing or to remain in a cramped hut for days on end. For females, restrictions are generally at the level of minimal social recognition, whereas for males they go beyond that to the level of personal dramatization.[2] This fact supports the generally held impression that female role recognition, in contrast to that for males, is more often accomplished by restriction than by prescription. This conclusion is further indicated by the fact that "ritual performances of the initiate" (an item similar to personal dramatization, step 2) are proportionately less frequent for girls than for boys.

A number of other attributes occur in some societies in association with dramatic sex-role recognition. Having a feast or hiring a specialist is somewhat more likely to occur for boys than for girls. This association is even more pronounced in the case of a loose category labeled "other emotional group responses," which includes sexual license at ceremonies, theatrical performances, showing of tabooed ritual paraphernalia, tossing the initiate into the air and threatening to let him fall, rubbing salt into a cut on the tongue or penis, and other similar practices.

Genital operations (clitoridectomy, circumcision, subincision, and superincision) were part of the girls' ceremony in only two societies and of boys' rites in nine. This item did not scale. But it would have been surprising had the mere fact of a particular operation been part of a sequence of social communication. Genital operations in themselves are not necessarily dramatic; thinking and social preparation make them so.

Performers, Setting, and Audience

If initiation ceremonies are to be handled in a dramaturgical framework, it should be possible to find empirical indicators of the "pro-

[2] For males this item is equivalent to step 2, with two errors. For females it cuts step 1 with three errors.

duction." Characteristics of the performers, the setting, and the audience should relate to degree of dramatization.

The age of initiates has already been mentioned. Although there are exceptions and the range is wide, most boys and girls are initiated at puberty in their early teens. The age range for girls appears narrower, perhaps because the onset of menstruation is a more obvious marker—although that varies too. An equally plausible reason, however, is that most girls are initiated individually. Thus there is no waiting for a year or more until a group of initiates is collected.

The findings on the number of initiates involved in the ceremonies are presented in Table 2. The size of each initiate group was coded simply as "usually one, but occasionally two," or else "a group of two or more." The ethnographies do not report this fact more precisely, and very likely there is a built-in relationship to the size of the local group and the length of time between ceremonies. Degree of dramatization is dichotomized in this table; steps 1 and 2 are contrasted with steps 3 and 4 because that division seemed to reflect the individual and group foci of the ceremonies. This simplification, however, does not negate the previous demonstration of an underlying continuum, with personal and group aspects present at both levels.

TABLE 2. **Number of Initiates by Degree of Dramatization for Males and Females**

| | DEGREE OF DRAMATIZATION | | | |
| | MALES | | FEMALES | |
	Low (*steps 1-2*)	*High* (*steps 3-4*)	*Low* (*steps 1-2*)	*High* (*steps 3-4*)
Usually one, but occasionally two candidates	67	0	85	54
Two or more	33	100	15	46
Total cases*	(12)	(10)	(20)	(11)

* In this and subsequent tables, the total number of cases may fall short because of lack of data.

Comparing males and females makes it apparent that the latter are typically initiated individually. This is true to a large extent even when some group response is made to the initiate. In contrast, when ceremony is elaborate, the social response made to males is almost invariably to a group of boys. Even at the lower level of dramatization boys are initiated in groups in about a third of the societies.

A prevalent aspect of girls' ceremonies that was difficult to analyze involves both the performers and the setting. It has often been remarked that the community attitude toward the menstruating initiate is one of revulsion, avoidance, and awe. While this is true in some societies, particularly in North America, it is by no means the predominant attitude, which tends toward admiration. The attitude toward the male initiate is almost always a positive one. The presence of such negative attitudes toward the female has often been attributed to a primitive "fear of blood" or "uncleanness," but such an explanation only begs the question. One hypothesis that encompasses all of these negative attitudes is that they operate as a functional equivalent of physical separation. No society lets young girls stray far from home, and it is relatively rare that girls are initiated in supervised groups outside the settlement. On the other hand, the rites often involve separation. The negative attitudes of the community toward a girl in a nearby menstrual hut would function quite well to give her a sense of isolation despite her physical proximity.

The duration of the ritual period is another aspect of the setting. The length of time during which a candidate is considered exceptional may be no more than a day, or it may extend over a year or more. In the latter case the ceremonies usually consist of a series of events each lasting a week or more, with the initiates remaining secluded during the intervals. Table 3 shows the relationship of the duration of the ritual period to the degree of dramatization.

As with the previous finding on numbers, boys are more likely to

TABLE 3. **Duration of Ritual Period by Degree of Dramatization for Males and Females**

| | DEGREE OF DRAMATIZATION | | | |
| | MALES | | FEMALES | |
	Low (*steps 1-2*)	High (*steps 3-4*)	*Low* (*steps 1-2*)	*High* (*steps 3-4*)
Up to a week	75	10	84	50
Week or more	25	90	16	50
Total cases	(12)	(10)	(19)	(10)

have long ceremonial periods at the higher level of dramatization, a result that is supported by the internal evidence of elaboration contained in the scales themselves. Still other indicators of elaboration have already been mentioned—feasts, presence of a paid specialist, and "emotionalized group responses"—all of which were more frequently associated with male initiations.

Another way to consider the setting is to ask what relationship, if any, the various organized groups in the community have to initiation rites. Webster (1938) has documented the association of secret societies with these rites of passage, but there are also nonsecret clubs, access to the men's house, and various war and raiding groups to be considered. If initiation ceremonies are dichotomized into those with "no apparent relationship to an organized group" versus those that are related (usually as a requirement of membership or full participation), then the results are as follows: female initiation rarely involves an organized group. In only one instance, that of the Samoans, was the principal ceremony for adolescent females the initiation or admission ceremony for a particular voluntary organization. A few other societies, like the Hopi and Dahomeans, have women's societies with entrance ceremonies, but the most elaborate ceremony, which was the one accepted for coding as an initiation, was not related to an organization. The initiation of boys was associated with participation in a definite group in five, or 23 per cent, of the cases. Such an association was more frequent for the more elaborate dramatizations.

These results have two sides. Insofar as initiation is connected with a particular organization, the ceremony will tend to be infused with the organizational purposes, which then become an important part of the setting. But if they are not so associated, as is true of nearly all the female and more than three-quarters of the male ceremonies, the possibility that initiation is simply a means of registering membership is eliminated. Whatever the function of initiation, it is more than an entrance requirement to a formal or informal group.

This research rejects education, in the sense of systemized communication of knowledge to young people, as a part of the setting of initiation ceremonies. Even in the longest ceremonial periods, the elders taught the initiates little more than myth and ritual and some moral precepts. But the pilot investigation indicated that even this was rare. Moreover, such teaching was inseparably a part of the dramatic components. Had it been a distinct part of the initiation activity, dramatization would have been deficient as a general concept. But the evidence of this sample is that the teaching that does occur is part of the "show" in the same sense that a practice like hazing is.

Turning to the audience, we encounter a problem of definition. Are the initiates themselves an audience? Perhaps not completely, but certainly they are when the elders are giving a performance of one kind or another. Indeed, for many dramatic events even women are allowed to watch. When the boys are considered performers and the adults of the community the audience, the number of adults is related to degree of dramatization, as shown in Table 4.

TABLE 4. **Size of Audience by Degree of Dramatization for Males and Females**

| | DEGREE OF DRAMATIZATION | | | |
| | MALES | | FEMALES | |
	Low (*steps* 1-2)	*High* (*steps* 3-4)	*Low* (*steps* 1-2)	*High* (*steps* 3-4)
Family or close friends only	50	20	78	36
Part or all of community	50	80	22	64
Total cases	(12)	(10)	(18)	(11)

Ethnographies do not contain accurate data on the number of observers, but it is usually possible to decide whether a ceremony is a family affair or whether a group larger than the family attends. Family groups may number ten to twenty people; if a larger group is present, there may be as many as 100 people, depending somewhat on the size of the local group. Table 4 is consistent with all the other evidence: A large audience is more likely when males are being initiated and when there is a high degree of dramatization.

Summary

The purpose of this chapter is to specify the phenomena under study so that a clear explanation and empirical tests can be undertaken.

The wide range of ritual customs that have been combined in various ways in different societies and focused on adolescents may be conceptualized as the dramatic forms of sex-role recognition. A measure of this dramatization is presented that arranges the practices in a unidimensional, cumulative sequence moving from minimal social recognition to affectively charged group rituals.

By this scale a greater proportion of societies dramatizes the sex role of girls, but the ceremonies for boys are more elaborate. The greater elaboration for males is further indicated by the association of a number of complex customs with a high degree of dramatization. Similarly related are other aspects that reinforce the notion of initiation as a social drama: the duration of the ceremony; the number of candidates; and the size of the audience.

2. The Functions of Male Initiation Ceremonies

Implicit in the definition of initiation ceremonies as dramatic forms of sex-role recognition is a commitment to a particular line of explanation. This theory makes more of the function of rituals for groups than for individuals, and it emphasizes the formal characteristics of ritual communication more than the content. Its central tenet is that ceremonies like initiation help to maintain the integration of particular social units. Sometimes the group is society in general, sometimes it is the community or the family. In the present case, it is the group that may be formed by all the adult males of a community.

When the men of a community cooperate to project a particular definition of their situation to an "audience"—to another group of men or to the women and children of the community—they may be said to show solidarity. This dimension of organization is always a matter of degree, but a crucial threshold occurs when all the men, not just a particular age group or status, must normally be involved in the activity and when such activity includes at least a thin consensus on a few beliefs. The typical elements in the male definition of the situation are that "men are quite different from women and uninitiated boys," that "men have particular and important activities to perform, such as keeping up the religion or making war," and that "all males must show loyalty to the group in word and deed." The concrete expression of solidarity may vary greatly, from veneration of a particular rock to participation in gang rape, but there must be some shared social meaning that is expressed in regularized ways.

This definition excludes the informal male solidarity present in all societies that is exemplified in separate male and female toilet practices, language differentiation, or variation in adornment. It also rules out the solidarity of the many voluntary or military organizations in modern society. If these did in fact include all the adult men of the society, as might happen with a total mobilization, the definition would be fulfilled. But, in general, the institutionalized, community-wide male solidarity which figures in this study occurs neither in very small communities, where informal patterns are adequate for delineating the division of labor, nor in larger differentiated communities, where community-wide consensus gives way to subgroup patterns.

It is customary in anthropology to stress the traditional or "given" nature of culture. So phrased, the conventional meanings held by the men are handed down and each new recruit must "conform to the norms." Cultural change in this view is brought about by innovators who change the body of tradition and thereby set new standards of conformity. In broad outline this image of man and culture assumes in the interplay between the individual and his tradition a relationship that is essentially antagonistic. Despite secondary emphasis on biological, personality, or historical factors and despite disclaimers that "no individual can arrive even at the threshold of his potentialities without a culture in which he participates" (Benedict 1948: 234), the basic assumption, to quote Benedict again, is that individuals "are plastic to the moulding force of the society into which they are born" (1948:235).

What is missing in the conformity model of man and culture is a consideration of the changing and emerging orientations that result from the coordination of social relations among the members of any group. Except for the workings of constitutional or unconscious factors or the efforts of "deviant" innovators, the theory gives little room to individual contributions like opinions, informal voting or pressures, strategems or multiple role-playing. The obvious facts of everyday adult life are tacitly denied.

Recently, however, Erving Goffman (1959) has stated the alternative position in the language of the drama. In his terms, the natural condition of man is to coordinate his efforts with those of others— sometimes the "other" of his own imagination—in order to project a particular impression to an audience. Such image-making develops in all sorts of groupings, from informal to formal associations. It is not that people are always putting on an act, but simply that life is more like a series of little shows than anything else that prompts Goffman's interpretation. Thus, a boy and girl cooperate for the benefit of a real or imagined audience to define their situation as one of courtship and love. While no one but a cynic would deny that they have really "fallen in love," only someone unsophisticated in modern sociology would doubt that their condition can be usefully construed as a more or less rehearsed performance, using the props and lines provided by their social class and strongly conditioned by the impression they are trying to create. Similarly, the gamut of social role behavior—from the burdens of high office to the cleaning woman's flurry of energy as the superintendent approaches—can be analyzed as interplay among constantly realigning teams of ever-changing participants.

The emphasis in this interpretation is on the "inside" of culture, on the way the participants create and maintain their view of the world. The referent is the group—a lone individual is a team with one participant—but the interpretation succeeds in presenting the individual contributions in a prominent way. Keeping up appearances is a dynamic process, and we are led to consider what happens when this work fails. In the case of a solidary team of adult males, the definition of their place and activities is constantly threatened by each new member of the cast. It is difficult to maintain consensus, often on subtle attitudes and beliefs, if each year or so a number of younger men are added. And if they are not added, the pattern of male activities is threatened even more.

A solution that solidary groups in all cultures have hit upon is to give a play within a play. In microcosm, the dominant themes of male solidarity are recreated in a setting that makes the initiates the central performers. In the crowded and emotionally charged situation that usually develops in initiations, the boy's thoughts are caught up. Even if he is not personally impressed, he still contributes to the performance simply by submitting to the ritual. But he cannot fail to realize one significant fact: For the first time in his life he is "backstage," looking at the women and the uninitiated from the standpoint of the men. Only death or a psychosis will return him to the audience.

From the point of view of the men the initiation is an orderly way of handling a potential disruption. The very fact that men do agree on certain tenets means that the coming of new members is a threat to their delicate consensus. And the greater the consensus, the greater the possibility that the ideas and actions of the recruits will dilute or change the particular structure of beliefs that the men maintain. It is not that a boy will argue or scoff at one thing or another; what is at stake is the very system of age-sex categories that makes it possible for the men to work together at all. It follows that any changes in the initiation ceremony will come about only when the men redefine their solidarity. If the community is threatened by war and the men have closed ranks in preparation for it, they may decide that tests of fortitude must be more exacting; if the men have reacted to the monotony of peace with a laissez-faire attitude, they may express by their disinterest in the preparations their view that male solidarity is not what it once was. Then the initiation practices become play and fashion among the young and fade from their serious role in society.

In this view the crucial determinant of dramatization is the degree to which the strongly held beliefs of the men articulate with one another to form a unified conception. It is the degree of coordination of points of view—not the homogeneity of belief. Since the male group is the relevant social unit, the content of these ideas will express a limited range of interests, but in those communities where the male view is the community view, this range of interests may serve for the women too.

A Functional Paradigm

Two important methodological advances that have come to the social sciences in the postwar period are the systemization of functional analysis and the routinization of comparative research. The second of these, in the particular form of comparisons based on the cross-cultural data contained in the Human Relations Area Files, is the basis of the subsequent chapters. But the tool of functional analysis may also help to clarify the line of theory that guides the comparisons.

The essential elements of functional analysis[1] are the assumptions that the system under consideration must meet certain conditions

---

[1] Even the recent literature on functionalism is extensive, but the following are more concerned with the underlying assumptions: Merton (1957:19-84), Nagel (1956:247-83), Hempel (1959:271-307), and Cancian (1960:818-27).

if it is to maintain an "adequate level" of operation; that the level of functioning can vary over wide limits from high integration to the termination of the system; that particular items of culture help to maintain a given level; and that items superficially different may operate as equivalents in their contribution to the maintenance of the ongoing system. This framework of assumptions has been given the following form by Carl Hempel (1959:287):

a. at time t, system s functions adequately in a setting of kind c
b. s functions adequately in a setting of kind c only if condition n is satisfied
c. therefore, some one of a particular class of cultural items is present in s at t

Inserting the concrete aspects of initiation ceremonies into this paradigm, we may say that the system in question is formed by the interaction of the adult males in the community. The class of cultural items is "initiation customs," which include particular items like gifts, tattooing, fasting, circumcision, seclusion, etc. The setting includes such preconditions of solidarity as the possibility of face-to-face interaction or the threat of war. Condition n, the functional requirement or need of the system, is in this case the maintenance of a minimum consensus regarding age-sex classifications, that is, male solidarity. Finally, the adequacy of functioning of the system is implied by the fact that the community was still operating when the ethnographer was there, or that at least there were some informants who could remember such a state of the system.

If it is true that the level of operation of social systems varies widely and that many functional equivalents exist for maintaining a system at a given level, then prediction of social events is limited to the weak form indicated in the paradigm. According to the syllogism, the best prediction possible is the *class* of cultural items within which alternatives occur. Whether or not such a restriction effectively inhibits social research is one of the underlying questions of this study.

The paradigm of functional analysis raises many other questions, and that is its virtue. Why not use the community or family as the system of reference? Why concentrate on the class of items defined as initiation customs when quite different classes, such as informal role recognition or a shift in the boy's sleeping quarters, may combine with initiation customs to form a more general class of "boundary-maintaining mechanisms"? Other questions arise with respect to the assumption that all social systems require a minimum consensus on role categories. Why choose a group-level statement of the assumption? Is it not more heuristic and faithful to common sense to emphasize the survival requirements of individuals rather than groups and to assume that all individuals need cognitive orientation if they are to function adequately? Indeed, the phrase "function adequately" in itself holds a question. What are the limits of adequacy for male solidarity, or for any system? When may we say that the male group has ceased to exist?

To answer these questions would be to compress into this chapter much of the discussion that develops later when these issues are concretely exemplified in the data. Perhaps, however, the bare statement of the solidarity hypothesis in the terms of functional analysis makes the central point: The framework clarifies the conceptual and empirical tasks.

The Function of Initiation for Individuals: A Group-Level Interpretation

Initiation ceremonies, whether simple or elaborate, seem to occur in communities in an all-or-none fashion. There is some mention in the ethnographic literature of the acceptance of particular customs—mainly circumcision—by only a part of the community, but this merely attests to the rapidity with which the practice is taken over in that community. Similarly, all the other group-wide ceremonies of this type—birth customs, marriages, funerals—seem clearly designed to apply to all normal members of the society. In primitive society the person who does not pass through the accepted rites of passage is usually abnormal.[2] Thus, whatever the contribution of initiation to the personality development of individuals, it is one that all boys require. What, then, is it?

[2] In commenting on his remarkable films of Australian aborigines, Norman Tindale, in a lecture at the University of California, mentioned a fatherless boy who, as the films clearly showed, was unusually frightened during the initiation. Even when one of the men acted as his "father," he was not reassured. The boy managed to get through the ceremony but died a few years later.

Again the definition of initiation has indicated the answer proposed in this study. All boys must learn their sex role. No society can allow this fundamental division of social labor to be too greatly blurred. But there are many variations in the social meaning of male status. In some societies being a hunter, a warrior, and a husband and father are all one, and the conditions of life, as among the Eskimo, are such that there is no need for special ritual delineation. In modern societies the organization of the modal roles is just the opposite. Family and occupational positions are not only differentiated from each other, but there is also great variation within each type. The communication of roles must therefore be more flexible, making use of formal education, mobility, and situational learning.

Between these two levels of complexity is a middle range where there is differentiation among roles, but little within them. Such societies have an organized occupational and family system, but there is little specialization within these structures. The roles have considerable "institutional freight" and must be accurately learned. But the assimilation cannot be left to the informal communication of growing up; definite social mechanisms are required. It follows from this picture of middle-level social structure that all rites of passage in a given community should be equally elaborate, but the present study deals with only two of them.

The function of initiation for the individual, then, is to reinforce a boy's ability to perform his sex role in that type of society that presents him with definite and institutionalized male status. He must learn the definition of the male situation maintained by the organized adult males. It is more than learning how to hunt or to plow, how to take heads, or how to deal with women. Rather, he must learn to view the world from the adult male standpoint. He must identify with the males by taking as his own their definition of events. And the greater the solidarity of the men, the more difficult this is without institutional help, because the men's world is tabooed to women and uninitiated boys. To use Goffman's terminology, they are not allowed in the male "back region," and yet it is only by being backstage that a boy can appreciate the full import of the male role.

The assumption here is that no individual can fully comprehend a symbolic environment in which he does not actually participate.

That is, he cannot learn to act unhesitatingly in accord with it unless he is part of it. There is much that goes on in the "back" of any organization that can never occur in the "front," where the team is engaged in projecting an image of itself. As Goffman puts it:

> . . . persons who co-operate in staging the same team-performance tend to be in a familiar relation to one another. This familiarity tends to be expressed only when the audience is not present, for it conveys an impression of self and teammate which is ordinarily inconsistent with the impression of self and teammate one wants to sustain before the audience. . . . The backstage language consists of reciprocal first-naming, co-operative decision-making, profanity, open sexual remarks, elaborate griping, smoking, . . . playful aggressivity and "kidding," inconsiderateness for the other in minor but potentially symbolic acts, minor physical self-involvements such as humming, whistling, chewing, nibbling, belching, and flatulence [1959:128].

In other words, the total range of adult male behavior is open to the boy only when he is allowed backstage and not until that time.

But there is still another kind of communication:

> When the members of a team go backstage where the audience cannot see or hear them, they very regularly derogate the audience in a way that is inconsistent with the face-to-face treatment that is given to the audience. . . . [It is] often ridiculed, gossiped about, caricatured, cursed, and criticized when the performers are backstage . . . [Goffman 1959:170].

Goffman goes on to suggest that the general function of the derogative treatment of the absent is to increase group solidarity, but in the present context what is to be emphasized is the opportunity for the boy to learn the male view of women.

Lack of maturity is an additional barrier to the male world. Until a boy is past childhood, he is not able to comprehend the symbolic environment, even though he may overhear the talk of his elders. Common observation suggests that the child only gradually accumulates the experience and the linguistic skill that enable him to make sense out of the going institutional structures of society. If adults are often confused in matters of sex, family life, religion, and authority, what must be the situation of the child? Probably even the most intelligent boy does not awaken to these complex meanings until early adolescence, and some take longer. Interestingly, the ethnographic accounts sometimes mention that a father decided that his son was "not ready" for initiation, even when the boy was older than other candidates. The basic reason for children's not comprehending adult communication is not, however, a lack of intelligence or even the inability to use correct forms of speech. It is that they are physically unable to interact at the adult level. They cannot procreate and they cannot do enough work. Therefore, they do not participate fully in the adult world.

Thus, the initiation ceremony helps the boy learn his sex role by placing him, once he is physically ready, in the appropriate sector of the social structure. It is not that he learns during this short period any significant knowledge, or even attitudes, nor is it adequate to say that the boy internalizes his role by experiencing a shift in status from the team that is not initiated to the team that is. Rather, the ceremony gives the boy access to another symbolic world. The men allow him backstage to their "show," and he is concomitantly barred from the doings of women. Now the real learning begins, and only a few significant experiences—such as hearing a man laugh at the women as he whirls the "terrifying" bull-roarer—are necessary before the boy understands a whole range of ideas that he only dimly perceived before. Then, as he emerges from the ceremony and its ritual seclusion, he immediately notices that the women and young boys treat him differently. He has previously been in their place and has implicitly learned the counterrole that he now takes as his own. In no time he adapts to the circumstance of being the "person" and thinking of the uninitiated as the "other." Under such conditions learning is swift, sure, and satisfying.

However, it is one thing to say that initiation ceremonies have an individual aspect and quite another to say that individual factors are causal. The psychological aspects of initiation are certainly present, but they are simply a part of the total process. In the technical terms of multivariate analysis, psychological factors would be controlled out by group-level factors, i.e., solidarity, but the former would not thereby be shown to be spurious or adventitious. On the contrary, the group-level factors can operate only through individuals, and the two levels form a developmental sequence.

Psychogenic Explanations

The solidarity hypothesis is a sociogenic explanation but, as the previous section argued, individual functions are not excluded. They are part of the total explanation; what happens to individuals is merely the obverse side of the group-level process. Homans (1941: 164-72) has pointed out this double aspect in his effort to harmonize the theories of Radcliffe-Brown and Malinowski, and there is no problem, according to Homans, if we realize that Radcliffe-Brown's emphasis on the institutional origin of anxiety—a pregnant woman is anxious because it is expected of her—is merely society's adaptation to the individual fact that one becomes frightened in new situations. But one suspects that Homans found harmony only by ignoring the many differences between sociogenic and psychogenic explanations. The fact is that Malinowski's explanation boils down to a group-level interpretation. In his famous example of lagoon versus sea fishing, where he points out that magic surrounds the more dangerous deep-sea enterprise, the emphasis is clearly on nonindividual factors. All the deep-sea fishermen observe magical practices; there is certainly no indication that the customs are confined to the timid men. Psychological factors are treated as constants; it is the situational factors that are explanatory.

We do not know how Malinowski might have developed his theory had he lived, but the works of such psychologically oriented theorists as Whiting[3] and McClelland (1961) illustrate a true psychogenic explanation. Their basic assumption is that factors that vary with individuals—anxiety, hostility, dependency, or achievement motivation—operate independently of situational factors in determining group-level phenomena. They probably would not deny that situational factors also operate or that social structure, like child-rearing prac-

[3] See especially Whiting (1961:353-80) and Burton and Whiting (1961:85-95). The reader should note that the sex-role hypothesis Whiting discusses in these papers is different from that proposed in the original article on initiation ceremonies (Whiting 1958:359-70). The first hypothesis used the close sleeping arrangement as an index of dependency; and another custom, a long postpartum sex taboo, was taken to indicate potential hostility. The function of initiation was to exert cultural control over these "potentially disruptive emotions." Inasmuch as sex-role conflict supersedes the earlier explanatory factor, discussion is confined to it.

tices, partly determines psychological tendencies, but they do deny that these tendencies may be treated as constants and that explanation may be couched purely in group-level terms.

Whiting's explanation of initiation ceremonies illustrates the psychogenic position. It begins with the effects on a child of its intimate relationship with its mother during the first years of its life. The concrete situation is an exclusive mother-child sleeping arrangement of the sort often found in polygynous families. According to Whiting, a boy develops an initial feminine identification as a result of the close maternal relationship, but later, if he grows up in a society where the rule of residence is patrilocal, the boy identifies with the men. The resulting sex-role conflict must be resolved with the aid of initiation ceremonies.

The basic explanatory mechanism is status-envy. Whiting postulates the arousal of envy in a person who perceives another as having more resources—food, prestige, capacity to give care, etc. And when envy develops, identification with the envied person follows. Thus, Whiting's hypothesis states a relationship between identification conflict in individuals and the occurrence of a community institution.

The hypothesis may be stated more formally as follows: If the social structure of a society operates to socialize a boy to both female and male roles, some institution will develop for resolving the conflict and reinforcing the male role, if the society is to survive. The conditions of this conflicting identification are to be sought in the "maintenance system" of the society, that is, in the organization of work and production. This in turn is hypothesized to influence the child-training practices that are the direct preconditions of sex-role conflict. In this particular hypothesis, Whiting uses the custom of a long and close mother-child sleeping arrangement as an indicator of female identification and the custom of patrilocal residence as an indicator for male identification. The conflict-resolving institution is, of course, the initiation ceremony.

As yet no explanation of girls' initiation ceremonies has been proposed, but Chapter 6 will discuss his parallel hypothesis that attempts to explain the "couvade." This institution is described as a way of handling the intense female identification that would arise if, in addition to the initial feminine identification during infancy brought about by such close association with the mother, the boy grew up in a matrilocal society—a situation that Whiting believes would further reinforce his feminine identification.

It is important to understand that these and other hypotheses are simply instances of a general framework that begins with the "maintenance system" but moves on to the related child-training practices and then to a class of dependent variables labeled the "projective system." That is, people are busy making a living and this prompts them to train their children in particular ways, depending upon the pressures and restrictions of subsistence. The socialization of the child sets up certain personality tendencies that predispose him to react in predictable ways to the religious, political, and cultural organization of the society. The typical reaction is conformity to and support of the beliefs of the society; and the task of the social scientist is to understand how particular kinds of maintenance customs determine the child-training practices that then determine the all-important personality tendencies and combinations that are taken to be central to the whole process.

While there are many aspects of this conceptual framework that fall outside the present discussion,[4] the present, more specific task is to analyze Whiting's sex-role conflict explanation of initiation ceremonies as an illustration of a class of "psychogenic" hypotheses. This type of explanation has had a great impact on attempts to explain social institutions, and the trend continues with current efforts to explain economic development in terms of the personality characteristics of entrepreneurs. If the issue were simply which of two explanations of initiation ceremonies is correct, the criticism and dissection of the sex-role conflict hypothesis scattered throughout these chapters would be quite out of proportion to the importance of the topic. But the problem is much broader, involving nothing less than two contrasting perspectives on the nature of society, one of which emphasizes the organization of tendencies within individual minds, acting in parallel, while the other focuses on the organization and interaction of the individuals as molar units.

Besides the choice of causal pattern, there are other contrasts in the

---

[4] The problem of the meaning of the ceremonies has already been taken up, and Chapter 8 will analyze some of the theoretical implications of the psychogenic position. There are also problems of method and empirical testing that are reviewed in Chapters 3 and 4, and the couvade hypothesis is submitted to a differential test in Chapter 6.

two types of explanation. Psychogenic theories typically assert, first, that personality trends are initiated in childhood and maintain themselves for many years before crucially determining some aspect of culture. Secondly, it is the unconscious determinants of personality that are held to be significant, to the degree that one might easily infer that the elaboration of initiation rites, whether originating within the society or borrowed, is managed without explicit conscious discussion or consideration by the men, or at any rate, that their deliberations are mere rationalizations. Third, psychogenic theories typically ascribe complicated processes to the average individual: not only does he project, repress, and make subtle comparisons and interpretations as a child, but he also nurses deep conflicts as he grows up. Fourth, and most pertinent to this study, person-specific explanations assume that tendencies in a portion of the community can determine the institutional participation of the whole group. Given the other assumptions, this one implies a kind of "drift" of many individual unconscious tendencies converging to predispose the community toward the elaboration of initiation rites. The model seems to be that of voting, but it would have to be unconscious voting. Using this framework, Whiting is able to show an association between male initiation ceremonies on the one hand and intimate mother-son sleeping arrangements and patrilocal residence on the other. But it is possible to ignore every one of these assumptions and explain the association, as Chapter 4 attempts to do, in terms of the solidarity hypothesis.

Alternative Group-Level Interpretations

The assumptions of psychogenic explanations contrast most sharply with those of the solidarity hypothesis, but there are other sociogenic explanations that vary in details. One of these is Radcliffe-Brown's. His basic account is contained in his book *The Andaman Islanders*,[5] ostensibly a report of field observations, but one which emerges as a key source in the line of social theory initiated by Durkheim. Some

[5] (Radcliffe-Brown 1948). E. Durkheim's *The Elementary Forms of the Religious Life* is perhaps the most relevant source for the initial conception.

of Radcliffe-Brown's interpretations of particular aspects of initiation ceremonies have already been mentioned, and it is clear from these that he sees the ceremony as a way of conveying to the initiate a sense of the important social values of the tribe. By highlighting social symbols, the ceremonies aid in the moral education of the young, teaching them to take their duties seriously. The initiate learns the importance of conformity to tribal customs and of respect for elders and the value of food. "The ceremonies teach the youth or girl to realize what is implied in being a member of the society by putting him or her during the period of adolescence in an exceptional position, and, as it were, outside the society" (Radcliffe-Brown 1948:278).

Later, in an article entitled "Taboo," he summed up his conception as follows:

> Briefly the theory is that the rites are the orderly . . . expression of feelings appropriate to a social situation. They thus serve to regulate and refine human emotions. We may say that partaking in the performance of rites serves to cultivate in the individual sentiments on whose existence the social order itself depends [1956:146].

In this account, Radcliffe-Brown assumes that the community as a whole is the system of reference. Also implicit, but only so, is the research hypothesis linking the degree of solidarity to the presence and elaboration of initiation rites. Radcliffe-Brown emphasized the different social values put on food, nature, and social life in primitive society, but he never had occasion to formulate a more specific hypothesis. Had he actually tested his theory empirically, as Durkheim did with respect to suicide, he could not have avoided a more precise formulation.

In contrast to the solidarity hypothesis, Radcliffe-Brown's account places more emphasis on the direct inculcation of society's precepts during the course of the ritual period. Whether this is in fact the case is a question that can be settled only empirically, but the general emphasis on the symbols of the ceremony is wholly acceptable. What the taboos on food and behavior convey is not specific knowledge, but generalized social attitudes of social welfare and self-control. Painting with white clay expresses a boy's exceptional status, and the responsive dance of the men affirms the solidarity of society. The general function of the symbols, both artifact and gesture, is to delineate for all concerned the boy's new social position.

In another version of Durkheim's thought, Chapple and Coon (1942:484ff.) explain rites of passage as ways of reequilibrating the social system. They combine the emphasis on the symbolic representation of the change in social relations with Van Gennep's typology of ritual phases and go on to a second hypothesis, that the different classes of rites—birth, initiation, marriage, death, etc.—vary in complexity and in the number and types of relations involved. "These differences depend on the magnitude of the changes, on the number of individuals and institutions affected, and on the degree to which they are affected as well" (Chapple and Coon 1942:506). Thus, the death of an adult is surrounded by more ceremony than the death of a child, and the death of a king involves more ritual complexity than either. Typically the death of a male involves more ceremony than that of a female because the degree to which the institution is affected—assuming male dominance—is greater. This statement is further explicated when it is understood that Chapple and Coon define an institution as a *group*, the interaction of which is equilibrated. It follows that, in an exclusively male group, interaction should be markedly disturbed by the entry of new members who are potentially capable of full participation.

Clearly Chapple and Coon's interaction explanation, particularly the last part of it, has much in common with the solidarity proposition. While it is difficult to say whether their definition of an institution is equivalent to the notion of solidarity, it will be apparent in subsequent chapters how much the interaction point of view has influenced the operational indicators of solidarity and related variables. A second influence is their more flexible handling of the systems to which the ritual is relevant. It is not always "society" that is affected; the family, and by extension other groups, may be the unit of analysis.

Still another variation of the Durkheimian emphasis on group integration is proposed by Nathan Miller. He stresses the relationship between the elaboration of initiation ceremonies and the presence of external threat.

> The initiation rites are persecuted with special vigor when the exclusive, personal interests of the group or class are threatened by

exigencies, such as initial contact with alien peoples, migration, de-population, threat of complete extinction or absorption into outside cultures, or the *Heimweh* provoked by a novel environment. The elders under these circumstances try to maintain group consciousness and custom largely through the extensive emotional and mental school-ing of the manhood ceremonies, because only in this way can the social heritage be perpetuated as a living thing [1932:49].

This hypothesis echoes the interpretations that have been made of nativistic or revitalization movements as reactions to stress (see, for instance, Linton 1943:230-40 and Wallace 1956:264-81), and the comparison reminds us that something more in the way of explana-tion is required in view of the fact that the usual outcome of external stress is the destruction of the primitive group. The logical difficulty is that it requires the elders, whose organization is presumably weak-ened, to coordinate their efforts toward increasingly elaborate initia-tion ceremonies. While such efforts might be possible in the early stages of threat, it is doubtful that the few years between the onset of stress and the destruction or change of the group are sufficient to account for the elaboration of ceremonies reported in many tribes. The solidarity hypothesis avoids this problem by relating the cere-mony directly to the cohesion of the group, without assuming that particular external factors will invariably lead to such cohesion. Those factors hypothesized to lead to solidarity—intercommunity raids, type of subsistence pattern, etc.—are internal factors and are much more moderate.

Essentially, however, the evaluation of Miller's hypothesis is an empirical matter. At best it would be difficult to test because the kind of external disruption he mentions is irregular and of a sort not usually detailed by the ethnographers. Even if it is described, there is the additional difficulty that the primitive society is typically destroyed by the very factors thought to be causal, with the result that there is a definite paucity of case material.

Some Extensions of the Solidarity Hypothesis

Chapple and Coon (1942:501) point out that most rites of passage deal with situations in the family. This is so because the family is the principal structural unit in native communities, and sometimes it is coextensive with the community. Only in more complex societies do religious, military, or voluntary associations develop and require special ceremonies. Thus, if the solidarity hypothesis is to be extended to other ceremonies typical of primitive society, we must look to the family as the probable social unit.

Even the initiation of girls is probably a function of family organization. It is infrequent that the women of primitive communities organize to the extent that the males do, and their restricted mobility tends to orient them to the domestic establishment. The precise focus of female solidarity in nonindustrial communities is something of an empirical matter, but there is no reason why the solidarity hypothesis should not apply. Insofar as women form solidary groups, even within the family structure, the dramatization of a girl's transition to full participation in the sex group should occur.

Besides male and female initiation ceremonies, this study deals with one other, the dramatization of parental role. The traditional term "couvade" is so convenient that, despite its many connotations of imitation by a husband of his wife's behavior at childbirth, it cannot be wholly rejected. However, it can be redefined for the purposes of this study in line with the theory and the appropriate cross-cultural indicators. The hypothesis would state a relationship between the solidary social unit and the dramatization of parenthood. Such a unit is the large corporate family. The effective operation of such families depends upon clear status categories for the constituent conjugal units. But in most primitive communities a marriage is not stable until a child is born, so it is this event that prompts the ceremony which communicates a couple's new status to the community and to the new parents themselves.

It would be instructive to apply the solidarity hypothesis to marriage and funeral ceremonies, but such investigation is outside the scope of this book. However, a line of intensive investigation emerges concerning the nature of solidarity itself. At the outset of this research it was not apparent that similarities in the organization of communities, male groups, and families would be so marked. Nor was it entertained that solidarity would be so intimately related to dramatization. Consequently, much of the material in the following chapters leads implicitly to this wider problem.

Summary

The central hypothesis of this study is that dramatization of status changes in a group are most elaborate when the solidarity of the group is great—that is, when there is a great deal of cooperation among the members for the purpose of creating and maintaining a stable definition of the situation. This hypothesis is applied specifically to the potential disruption of consensus and solidarity in a group of men when boys are taken into it. The dramatization of sex role—initiation rites—is functionally necessary for maintaining the solidarity of the men. Such ritualization calls attention to the boy's change in status and gives him access to the intimate communication of the group. In this new social sector, the boy quickly consolidates his role and the stability of the community's age-sex status classification is preserved.

The same hypothesis should hold for dramatization of the female sex role and ritual recognition of parental status at the birth of a child. However, in the latter case it is the family that is the point of reference, rather than the adult members of one or the other sex.

Related concepts and cognate hypotheses were reviewed from the point of view of similarities and contrasts with the solidarity hypothesis, itself an elaboration of one strand of the theory initiated by Durkheim. The hypothesis depends especially on Goffman's dramaturgical framework, and it diverges significantly from psychogenic explanations of cultural phenomena, which stress the independent causal efficacy of individual-level factors.

3. Method of Study

One of the advantages of cross-cultural research based on the material contained in the Human Relations Area Files[1] (hereafter abbreviated HRAF) is that different investigators can use exactly the same cases, even for testing opposing hypotheses. This advantage may outweigh the fact that the original ethnographic reports were not collected from the point of view of any particular hypothesis and are therefore often inadequate or uneven. Thus, methodological discussion has a double task, that of maintaining the inherent strategic advantage of the stable data source and at the same time of finding acceptable ways to avoid or surmount its deficiencies. Because of this situation, considerations of method and technique will continue to take high priority in cross-cultural studies.

The Sample and Units of Analysis

This study began as a counteranalysis of an explanation of initiation ceremonies proposed by Whiting, Kluckhohn, and Anthony (1958).[2] Consequently, it used the sample of societies that they drew and that they describe as follows:

> First, the ethnographic material on more than 150 societies was checked to determine whether or not there was an adequate description of our variables, e.g., sleeping arrangements, *post-partum* sex

[1] An early description of this systematic body of ethnographic data is contained in Murdock (1961:45-54).
[2] The reanalysis is contained in Young (1962).

taboo, and initiation rites at puberty. Only half of the societies reviewed fulfilled these conditions. Although we had initially endeavored to select our cases so as to have maximum distribution throughout the world, we found that some areas were represented by several societies, while others were not represented by any. To correct for any bias that might result from this sample, we made a further search of the ethnographic literature in order to fill in the gaps, and we thereby added several societies from areas previously not represented. Finally, to maximize diversity and to minimize duplication through selection of closely related societies, whenever there were two or more societies from any one culture area which had the same values on all our variables, we chose only one of them. Using these criteria, our final sample consisted of 56 societies representing 45 of the 60 culture areas designated by Murdock.[3]

The societies comprising our final sample range in size and type from small, simple, tribal groups to segments of large complex civilizations such as the United States or Japan. In the latter case, our information has been drawn from ethnographic reports on a single delineated community [Whiting, Kluckhohn, and Anthony 1958:363].

This is a fair example of current cross-cultural sampling techniques, which, most investigators would agree, have many difficulties. Even in these paragraphs a number of them emerge: the lack of a parent population from which to sample, the problem of finding societies that are "independent" for statistical purposes, the lack of data relevant to the investigator's hypothesis, and the kind of unit that is to be sampled. Since the present study had to live with this sample, a searching analysis of its characteristics is in order. It is one's duty in cross-cultural research to look a gift horse in the mouth.

Beginning with the less difficult problems first, what was the unit of analysis? Were we sampling cultures, societies, or some smaller unit? In the present case, there was a straightforward answer: this was a sample of communities in the broad sense of autonomous, or nearly autonomous, locality groups. For large countries, such as the United States or Japan, there was no question; the ethnography is explicitly concerned with a particular community. But close examination indicates that this is also true of the "tribal" studies. The ethnographer

[3] Reference is to Murdock (1957:664-87). In many respects the data on these 565 societies are for anthropologists what the U.S. Census is for sociologists. [Author's note.]

typically focuses on one community, usually the one in which he spent most of his time. If he surveys a wide area, he typically organizes his report around one or more community-types, such as town and rural, or coastal versus inland. Thus, in terms of what ethnographers actually do, one usually has no choice but to study locality groups.

The present research would have had no option on this point anyway because the key variables of the study apply directly to communities and vary markedly with their characteristics. The acceptance of data from any part of a report or from ethnographies of non-locality groups would have introduced new variables and much extraneous information. For this reason the study sample dropped the two cases in Whiting's sample that were not communities—the Druze of Lebanon and the Rajput caste of a town in North India—to reduce the total to 54. Then from these 54 societies only the data relevant to a particular community or community-type were used.

Table 5 lists the study sample by continental areas, indicating the precise village whenever possible. If the report did not name a village, some description of the type of unit may be given. When the report was unspecific but seemed to concern only one type of locality group or one band without a group name, only the data of that particular field study were used. It was assumed that the restriction on diversity of sources insured homogeneous data. Even so, this study was unable to handle adequately a question already posed by Whiting (1954:26): When should large families living in isolated compounds or hamlets be considered communities in themselves rather than sub-units of a loose regional network that might be labeled the community? Because one's judgment on this problem depends so much on the particular question at hand, further discussion is left to the relevant chapters. For sampling and coding purposes, most isolated family-communities were accepted as units in this study. The population estimates in Chapter 5 reflect this judgment. ·

In addition to delimiting the unit of analysis in terms of its gross structural characteristics—whether it is a community, a tribe, a caste, etc.—one must fix the group in time. Small communities change radically in the course of a generation, and sometimes they disappear altogether. Therefore, the sample communities are identified in Table 5 by the approximate date to which the data apply. One consequence of this time placement was to restrict the investigation to relatively few sources, since it is infrequent that many ethnographers study a

TABLE 5. **Location and Time Period of the Study Sample**

Africa

Ashanti (peasants)   1920
Azande   1920
Chagga (Machame area)   1910
Dahomeans (Abomey)   1931
Egyptians (Silwa)   1951
Ganda (peasants)   1900
Lamba (Mushili district)   1917
Nuer   1928
Nyakyusa (Nu Ngonde)   1936
Pondo (Tibane)   1933
Tallensi (rural)   1934
Thonga (northern clans)   1910
Tiv   1920

Circum-Mediterranean and Europe

French (Peyrane)   1950
Lapps (nomadic in Sweden)   1875
Serbs (Orasac)   1953

East Eurasia

Japanese (Suye mura)   1936
Koryak (maritime)   1900
Lakhers (especially Savang)   1926
Lepchas (Lingtem)   1937
Tanala (Menabe)   1926

Insular Pacific

Alorese (Atimelang)   1938
Balinese (Belaluan)   1930
Bontoc Igorot (Bontoc)   1903
Fijians (Tokalau)   1934
Kwoma (Rumbima)   1936
Malaita (bush group)   1933

Maori (North Island)   1850
New Ireland (Lesu)   1930
Ontong Javanese (Luaniua and Pelau)   1928
Ooldea   1941
Samoans (middle class in Manua)   1926
Trobrianders (Omarakana)   1917
Trukese   1947
Yap (Fal)   1948

North America

Cheyenne (northern)   1850
Chiricahua   1870
Eskimos (Copper Eskimos around Coronation Gulf)   1914
Hopi (Hotavila)   1938
Kwakiutl (Fort Rupert)   1900
Mexicans (Tepoztlán)   1945
Mixtec (Santo Domingo)   1955
Navaho   1943
Ojibwa   1850
Papago (Hichwian and Gu Vo)   1942
United States (Homestead)   1950

South America

Araucanians (Cautinche)   1948
Cagaba   1947
Camayura (Juatuare)   1948
Jivaro (Achuare group)   1922
Pilaga   1936
Siriono   1940
Timbira (Ramcocamecra)   1932
Yagua   1940

specific community at the same time. Also, when a given source described two time periods equally well, the sample accepted the earlier account[4] to try to offset the obvious bias toward recent accounts present in Whiting's sample (this bias and its importance are dis-

[4] Sources for the Study Sample, pp. 182-88, and Sources for the Auxiliary Study, pp. 189-92, give complete citations for the ethnographic data of this study.

cussed in detail below). It should be noted that the more rigorous specification of the sample units in time may have led to some of the differences in the results of the two studies. The requirements of this study made it necessary to refine the sample, however, and the amount of change so introduced, although unknown, seems slight.

The problem of data adequacy is inherent in cross-cultural work. It will probably always be handled either by selecting for adequate material, as Whiting and his associates did, or by drawing a large sample for which data are generally adequate, and then accepting a large case loss.[5] After this, however, one must study the final sample for the biases introduced by the selection or loss. For instance, the interest of Whiting *et al.* in rather obscure child-training situations almost certainly biased his sample, and therefore the study sample, toward recent ethnographies written by field workers interested in family and socialization. At any rate, it seems improbable that 57 per cent of a sample drawn for any other purpose would consist of communities studied since 1930 and investigated, for the most part, by American ethnographers interested in "culture and personality." Because of the recency of these reports, about a third of the sample communities are modernized in the sense that the native children attend formal coeducational schools. And this particular institution, it turns out, has a marked negative effect on the occurrence of initiation ceremonies. In view of this probable bias, any interpretations that depend on the clustering of these modernized communities must be considered with skepticism.

The problem of independence of cases has haunted cross-cultural studies from the time of Tylor's first study. On the face of it the objection is strong. If, for instance, circumcision has basically three points of origin, from which other cultures borrowed the custom, then cross-cultural comparisons, no matter how many cases in the sample, boil down to three independent cases. This criticism has kept comparative studies on the defensive for a long time, and a great deal of time and thought has been devoted to meeting the objection (for instance, in Whiting 1954:528 and Naroll 1961:217-41). The description of Whiting's sample mentions his efforts to distribute the cases over the 60 culture areas of Murdock's World Ethnographic Sample, and

[5] This is one of the proposals in Driver (1961:325).

this is a common practice. Table 6 shows, however, that some regional bias crept in despite this precaution. The number of cases from
the Circum-Mediterranean European and East Eurasian areas seems
disproportionately low.

TABLE 6. **Comparison of Study and HRAF Auxiliary Samples by
Area Distribution**

*Continental areas of world ethnographic sample**	*Total study sample*	*Male initiation sub-sample (study sample)*	*Auxiliary male initiation sub-sample (HRAF)*
Africa	24	27	36
Circum-Mediterranean and Europe	6	0	0
East Eurasia	9	0	4
Insular Pacific	26	37	24
North America	20	18	24
South America	15	18	12
Total cases	(54)	(22)	(25)

* The number of societies in the World Ethnographic Sample located in each of
these areas was intentionally equalized, so no comparison is possible.

The second and third columns of the table throw further light on
this area distribution. The second column gives the area classification
of the 22 societies in the study sample that have male initiation ceremonies, as defined by the scale of dramatization. The HRAF subsample in the third column is a 50 per cent systematic random sample
of the 60 societies in the file that have male initiation ceremonies. The
impossibility of localizing the data in space and time resulted in a
loss of 5, bringing the actual number of cases to 25. The universe consists of the 211 bodies of data in the files that pertain to a single
social unit (in contrast to categories like "Baltic countries").

When the two initiation subsamples are compared with respect to
area distribution, they turn out to be quite similar. The highest proportions of initiation ceremonies for males occur in Africa and the
Insular Pacific, and the analysis in Chapter 5 of the subsistence factors
related to initiation explains why this is so. But this association does
not justify the bias toward Africa and the Insular Pacific—now quite

apparent—that appears in the total study sample. Again we are alerted to the necessity for procedures that will not build in area biases.

However, the foregoing discussion has strayed from the problem at hand. The purpose of controlling for culture areas is to meet the diffusion objection, but in practice the more pressing problem seems to be to control for the variables of social structure that are associated with these areas. Indirectly, of course, diffusion and social factors are inextricably related. It is generally assumed that traits diffuse to areas where they are best adapted, and adaptation in turn depends upon the exploitive organization that already exists in the region. Given this interdependency of diffusion and structures—a situation long recognized by anthropologists—it is at once apparent that the objection can be turned around. Is it not up to the diffusionists to show that their principles hold independently of the organization of the recipient society? When we consider the very weak evidence available in support of the diffusion of patterns of social relationships[6] and the fact that most of the variables of cross-cultural studies are complex structures, it seems reasonable that the burden of proof should shift to the diffusionists.

However, the present study had a special advantage in being able to side-step much of this debate. The variables used here are not merely patterns of social relationships, they are quite formal patterns. In many cases the content of the variable is quite diverse and could have been acquired from many sources. How can diffusion be a problem, for instance, when a given step of a scale may include a drinking session, a gift, or permission to have a sexual spree?

A fourth common problem is determining the population to which the sample may be generalized. Does the conclusion hold for all known or unknown human communities? Or just those studied by anthropologists? The problem was further complicated in the present sample by the use of the community as a unit: most ethnographers do not explicitly choose a locality group as the focus of study, and other research studies have drawn samples that were intended to be of "cultures" or "societies." It is a fair question, then, whether a "universe of human communities" is a reasonable ideal. At any rate, the present sample of 54 communities or community-types cannot be defended as representative of anything and is similar in this respect

[6] More correctly, the negative evidence; see Murdock (1949:240).

to most cross-cultural samples. However, it is instructive to compare the study sample to two possible universes: the 211 units in the Human Relations Area Files, which may be taken as a universe of well-described groups, and the 565 cases in Murdock's World Ethnographic Sample, taken as a universe of usable and diversified ethnographic data.

For instance, if the two male initiation subsamples in Table 6 are compared with respect to the degree of elaboration of the initiation ceremonies characteristic of each, there is a sharp difference. Sixty per cent of the HRAF auxiliary subsample is very elaborate (steps 3 and 4 of the dramatization scale), while only 44 per cent of the study subsample is.[7] The indication is that the HRAF units are biased toward well-studied, well-institutionalized groups. Cultures that are "thin" or in a stage of disintegration do not usually appear in this set of records. It may also be, though this is less probable, that the ceremonies with minimal elaboration were not recognized as such by the HRAF classifiers and that the data were not placed in the category (881, Puberty and Initiation) in which one would ordinarily expect to find them.

Another comparison points up the difference between the study sample and the HRAF universe. It will be recalled from Chapter 1 that 60 per cent of the study sample had no male initiation ceremonies according to the scale definition. This compares to 72 per cent in HRAF. Such a proportion is not surprising considering that about 38 per cent of the HRAF units consist of peoples of Asia and Europe, areas where modernization and complex social structure have eroded any initiation ceremonies that might once have existed.

Comparison to the World Ethnographic Sample must be made in terms other than initiation ceremonies. Although many different bases are possible, Table 7 shows the contrasts with respect to a typology of subsistence patterns and polygyny. In terms of subsistence differences, the study sample is biased toward modern groups that use imported animals and grow cereal crops. The previously mentioned bias of the study sample toward recently studied groups and the

[7] It must be remembered that the study sample includes many cases from the Human Relations Area Files, but they were not drawn in a systematic way, and other cases were added to them. In contrast, the "HRAF subsample" is representative of all the sources in the file.

acknowledged bias in Murdock's work toward aboriginal patterns like polygyny is further evidence of this contrast.

TABLE 7.   **Comparison of World Ethnographic and Study Samples by Subsistence Type and Marriage Pattern**

Comparison factor	World ethnographic sample	Study sample
Modern agriculture	5	15
Traditional agriculture	45	33
Horticulture	24	35
Gathering	26	17
Total cases	(565)	(54)
General polygyny (above 20 per cent)	41	30
Limited polygyny	33	37
Monogamy	23	33
Polyandry	1	—
No data	2	—
Total cases	(565)	(54)

In sum, the study sample of 54 communities cannot be generalized to any available universe. However, its particular biases in favor of modernized groups and communities with minimally elaborated initiation ceremonies will be shown to work to the advantage of later analysis. It was possible to control for these biases and at the same time to make use of the additional range of variation that was inadvertently introduced.

Data Collection and Coding

The procedures used in processing cross-cultural data are fairly well known so that all that is necessary here is a brief outline, with special emphasis on differences. After the investigator chose the particular community and era for each of the societies listed in the sample, coders searched the whole source for the items required by the data-collection schedule. They did not depend upon the HRAF categorizations or upon preliminary extraction of data. While it is not denied that precategorization is extremely useful for many purposes, there were two disadvantages for the present study. First, the HRAF categories are organized by content, so that it would have been possible to miss certain types of formal information even if a range of categories was searched. Moreover, when the whole source was used, one part of the report often helped the coder to understand details of other parts. Second, precategorization can result in an inflated measure of reliability. It is much more difficult to get agreement between coders when they search an entire source than when they are arbitrarily restricted to a few pages of data.

In the course of two years' work two different schedules were completely coded and tested. In addition, many hours of special studies and reliability checks preceded the work on each schedule. The data from schedule I proved adequate for testing the central variables of male solidarity and initiation, and one report (Young 1962) was prepared from that material. It is the data from schedule II, however, that form the basis of this book; it included all the successful categories from the first schedule and added more items on solidarity and the dramatization of parenthood. Ultimately, schedule I and the HRAF auxiliary subsample were considered together as the pilot study; in particular, the HRAF subsample served as an intensive pretest of schedule II.

An important result of this pretesting was the development of a style of coding that was reliable and was also consistent with the kind of theory used here. This approach to coding may be described briefly as the use of institutionalized cultural bits. That is, the schedules required the coders to hunt for data that were group level, either in the pure sense that a church indicates religious activity in the community or in the normative sense that a community with 20 per cent of the families polygynous probably has a general tendency toward polygyny as a form of marriage. Curves of individual variation, such as the harshness of toilet training by parents, were not accepted.

These "social facts" were coded without regard to the native meaning or to the meaning they might have in common-sense Western terms. However, the items had to have meaning in a certain minimal sense—they had to be recognized by the natives as stable parts of the symbolic environment. For instance, if a missionary had no following in a native community and appeared to be isolated, his activity was interpreted as outside the symbolic environment of the community and the item coded absent. Similarly, an item like "close and exclusive sleeping arrangement of mother and child" was rejected because it is probably only a spatial by-product of other customs and has in itself no cultural status. All this followed from the basic definition of social theory used in this study and generally in the social sciences.

This basic rule operated to increase the reliability of the coding. Since the reporting of institutionalized items varies less with the interests of particular ethnographers than does that of noninstitutionalized items, it meant, first, that the variables tended to incorporate only typically recorded data. Institutionalized customs may also be reported differentially, of course, but this happens less often because they stand out in any community and because the traditional anthropological categories have tended to emphasize such customs. Secondly, the rule also helped the coders to make reliable decisions about what to accept or reject. Thus, if men and women eat separately at some meals as a result of the men's work schedule, as in Tepoztlán, the item "sexes separated while eating in domestic establishment" was not checked. On the other hand, a post-partum taboo lasting only one month, the cultural status of which is attested by a belief that sexual intercourse sours the mother's milk, is coded as present.

Most of the preliminary research time was given over to finding institutionalized cultural activities that were relevant to the hypotheses and could be reliably combined into more complex scales or typologies. For this reason, the usual measuring of agreement between coders on particular items was unfortunately limited for these data. Some 15 cases of schedule I and about 20 of the HRAF auxiliary subsample were coded by two coders and then discussed. On the basis of this discussion and computations of reliability (before discussion) on small batches of eight or ten cases, the schedules were cut or revised until about 83 per cent agreement was regularly attained and the errors appeared random and owing to carelessness rather than to a deficiency of the coding rules. Unreliable items tended to be noninstitutionalized practices, customs—like dance patterns or men's games—that were difficult to find in a routine search, or detailed social relationships—like the organization of work parties—that are outside the traditional anthropological data-collection categories. In general, if an item was not usually found in a section of the ethnography that is labeled either in the Table of Contents or in chapter sections of one third or more of the reports, it was not likely to be reliable.

The coding of the study sample was the final stage in this long process. Ten cases of schedule II—about one-fifth of the total study sample—were compared and the reliability was found acceptable, but the main defense of these items must be that the hypotheses that incorporate them hold despite random variation.[8]

The Construction of Measures

Besides the basic emphasis on institutionalized social forms, two rules guided the construction of the various measures. The first was that all combinations of items had to accord with explicit procedures imposed after the initial coding. The second was that the relationship between the concrete indicator and the concept that it indexed must have a direct linkage.

The first requirement rejected the practice of rating or global coding. Even though two coders might have agreed on a number between one and seven that reflects a community's "typical" position on some variable like "general pressure for obedience," we could never know what actually went into the coders' judgment. It was not sufficient to instruct coders to consider such and such situations from a certain point of view; the procedure must guarantee that when fatigue and stereotyping set in, they did not simply code in place of the variable under consideration the degree to which a family is extended or whether the community herds cattle or makes use of wild plants. The only way to ensure that coders did not "build in" gross structural differences when coding subtle trends was to restrict them to particular items and combine these later. Such a procedure has the additional advantage of being more easily communicated to other investigators. What, after all, does "diffusion of nurturance" or "dependence satisfaction potential" mean operationally, even if one accepts the learning-theory derivation of these concepts?

After discrete cultural forms are coded, there are, unfortunately,

The complete study code is to be found in *Appendix A: Study Code*, pp. 165-71.

only a few ways in the present state of knowledge in which they may explicitly and legitimately be combined (i.e., without building in a larger meaning, such as hedonism or sex). Often it is best to treat them separately. It may be possible, however, to construct a typology by combining two or more attributes, as was done for the subsistence types discussed in Chapter 5 and as Murdock did for kinship terminology. A third possibility involves the ordering of attributes to form a cumulative, or Guttman, scale. Since this particular technique was frequently used in this study, some detailed discussion is in order.

Table 8 presents four of the items finally accepted in the dramatization scale, already described in Chapter 1. For illustration purposes, seclusion, an item not ultimately used, was inserted between the first and third items; the residual category of the final scale, nondramatic sex-role recognition, was omitted. Inspection shows that there are no errors except for the one introduced by the seclusion item. The Dahomeans do not practice seclusion even though they have all the other "higher" customs. Actually, one error does not require the rejection of an item; seclusion was dropped from the final scale because it entailed too many errors in the female scale and in the HRAF auxiliary subsample. Table 8 shows, moreover, that it did not discriminate between the first and third items and therefore added nothing to the efficiency of the measure. Perhaps with more sensitive coding of more cases and attention to functional equivalent of seclusion, the item would scale.

There are a number of other rules for assessing Guttman scales,[9] but all but two of the scales in this book have so few items that they do not qualify as true scales. At best they are approximations, and they are used here tentatively and with great reliance on external validation. More rigorous work may either extend these or result in other scales. If so, they will increase the efficiency of cross-cultural studies. It is easy to see that they would ensure coding reliability; any marked unreliability would result in so many scale errors that the item could not be used. Furthermore, once a scale is found, it can often be applied to a second batch of less adequate data. If an ethnography, for example, reports only that initiates are beaten in initiation camps, we can nevertheless be fairly sure that all the less elaborate aspects of

---

[9] These are incorporated in Herbert Menzel's coefficient of scalability, which is the measure applied to the scales reported here. See Menzel (1953).

8. Scalogram of Items in Dramatization Scale for Males (Nonscale item—seclusion—inserted)

COMMUNITY	Minimal social recognition	Seclusion	Personal dramatization	Organized social response	Affective social response	
Hopi	1	1	1	1	1	
Kwoma	1	1	1	1	1	
Ooldea	1	1	1	1	1	
Thonga	1	1	1	1	1	
Timbira	1	1	1	1	1	(5)
Azande	1	1	1	1		
Dahomeans	1	0	1	1		
Kwakiutl	1	1	1	1		
New Ireland	1	1	1	1		
Nuer	1	1	1	1		(5)
Balinese	1	1	1			
Cagaba	1	1	1			
Camayura	1	1	1			
Chagga	1	1	1			
Fijians	1	1	1			
Jivaro	1	1	1			
Ojibwa	1	1	1			
Tiv	1	1	1			(8)
Cheyenne	1					
Ontong Javanese	1					
Samoans	1					
Yap	1					(4)
Item errors	0	1	0	0	0	
Total cases						(22)

dramatization are present, since the original scale construction depended upon the cumulation of the items.

When attributes are combined into cumulative sequences, these sequences, or scales, facilitate the study of concomitant variation. Such scales, of course, are not as efficient as a simple yardstick, where one is sure that the intervals are equal, but they do make relative comparisons possible. Cross-cultural studies have suffered from an overemphasis on the presence or absence of attributes, a procedure that allows far too much latitude for error. Perhaps the use of explicit scaling techniques and associations showing concomitant variation will help to increase the sensitivity of hypothesis-testing in anthropological studies.

A third asset of Guttman scales helps to implement the second rule mentioned above, that the measures show a direct relationship to the concept. It is assumed that each item that is hypothesized to fit a scale will be coded without imputing a meaning to its content. Thus, hazing of an initiate may be coded "social attention of one sort or another" but not "punishment" or "show of authority"; the latter meanings involve complex hypotheses that must be tested explicitly and not left to the unchecked impressions of coders. A test is then made of the scale hypothesis by ordering the items, if possible, into a cumulative sequence. The hypothesis asserts degrees of elaboration or intensity of cultural forms, but it is still not possible to make more than a tentative interpretation of the meaning of the content. However, some hypotheses as to meaning can be rejected at this point. If, for example, a wide variety of parental observances and restrictions at the time of childbirth are found to scale, and if the particular items and the sequence contradict an interpretation along the lines of "imitation by the husband of wife's pregnancy," then further hypothesizing about the antecedents of such imitative behavior is out of order.

Ultimately, however, the establishment of a direct link between index and concept is a matter of analysis. A direct link is one that requires only the assumption of isomorphism; it does not assume a hypothetical mechanism. For instance, the dramatization scale requires only the assumption that the items reflect a particular way of communicating; in contrast, the interpretation of a custom like genital operations or hazing as one component of a reidentification process depends upon the acceptance of the hypothesis that the candidate reacts in some way to these customs so that his male identification is strengthened. Again, the link between a close mother-son sleeping arrangement and feminine identification requires, according to Whiting, the hypothesis that the child reacts with envy to his perception of the mother's status as dispenser of resources.

But such hypotheses are almost a research in themselves. The link assumes mechanisms and conditions not open to the reader's inspection. It is easy to see that the use of such "indicators" (or preconditions, as they should be called), linked only remotely to the concepts, opens the door to all sorts of biases and confusion. The analytical ice is thin enough when we assume that a particular item is a legitimate example of a certain class of phenomena, like dramatization or solidarity; it is absolutely untrustworthy when we assume a whole body of theory and evidence in order to justify the link.

A final relevant characteristic of scales is that they usually measure a formal dimension of social structure, such as intensity, elaboration, or development. They meet the requirement of abstraction necessary for cross-cultural variables, and in some cases they elucidate the interpretation of the temporal sequence of a given phenomenon. Both these characteristics are prominent in the scale of community-national articulation presented in Chapter 5 and will be discussed in detail in the empirical context.

Tests of Person-Specific and Group-Level Hypotheses

If the data of ethnography resist attempts by the researcher to operationalize his concepts, they are downright intractable when these concepts refer to individual-level constructs—so much so that it will probably never be possible to make adequate tests of person-specific hypotheses. These were characterized in Chapter 2 as asserting the independent causal efficacy of individual-level factors such as motives, capacities, or patterns of reaction. The difficulties become clear if the causal sequences of Whiting's sex-role conflict hypothesis are diagramed, as in Figure 1. For one thing, the causal sequence moves from the group level to the individual level and then back to the group level. This involves theoretical problems that have already been discussed.

A more concrete problem is to find adequate indicators for the individual-level phenomena. These indicators are tenuous in several respects. First, the global appraisal by ethnographers of such phenomena as exclusive mother-child sleeping arrangements cannot be trusted. They infrequently collect data on each household, and they have no other way of judging the uniformity of such a pattern without it. Second, as was previously argued, the indicator is quite indirect. It is a major theoretical and empirical problem in itself to move from mother-son interaction to intraindividual tendencies. To assume such a relationship is wholly gratuitous, and to assume that the mechanism works uniformly for all boys is even more dubious. Third, if uniform exposure of each boy is not considered necessary to the explanation— although it is difficult to imagine how this is possible within the Whiting framework—a new problem develops. If only some of the boys are exposed to the sleeping arrangement, which group determines the initiation ceremony? We lack evidence that the exposed boys do. Perhaps the boys who do not sleep close to their mothers are predisposed to support initiation ceremonies.

FIGURE 1. **Contrast in Causal Sequences of the Sex-Role Conflict and Solidarity Hypotheses**

sex-role conflict hypothesis

GROUP LEVEL:	Maintenance system (*polygyny*)	(*Exclusive mother-son sleeping arrangement*)	(*Patri-local resi-dence*)	Resolution mechanism (*initiation customs*)
INDIVIDUAL LEVEL:		Female ⟷ identi-fication	Male → identi-fication	Sex-role conflict

solidarity hypothesis

GROUP LEVEL:	Ecological de- ⟷ terminants (*col-lective hunting, warfare, etc.*)	Solidarity ⟷ (*scale of group-level items*)	Dramatization (*scale*)
INDIVIDUAL LEVEL:		Attitudes of loyalty, im-portance, etc.	Crystallization of male role

NOTE: An empirical indicator of a concept is enclosed in parentheses and placed in the same column as the concept. If the indicator and the concept are separated by the line dividing the levels, a substitution of group- for individual-level data has been made. Arrows indicate causal sequence. Double-headed arrows are reciprocal relationships. Broken-line arrows indicate the presence of a psychological aspect, which, however, is not causal.

In contrast, the solidarity hypothesis is completely phrased in group-level terms, and the indicators are group-level items. It is assumed that solidarity and dramatization have a psychological aspect (indicated by broken-line arrows), and data are admittedly lacking on these points. But pinning down these phenomena is not so crucial to the proof of the hypothesis as it would be for the individual-level reactions that are contained in the Whiting explanation. However, the solidarity hypothesis does include the following assumptions: (a) All individuals can learn and change as they interact in regular ways with significant others; (b) a strong and clear stimulus is learned more readily than one lacking these characteristics, and since dramatizations are strong, clear stimuli, they are readily learned; (c) given an initial exposure of equal impact, the variation in ability to learn and in sensitivity to stimuli is similar from community to community; (d) uniform exposure of the relevant individuals is more readily accomplished in solidary or dramatization situations.

Thus, by the very nature of its concepts and indicators the solidarity hypothesis contains a built-in control on individual variation. Moreover, the assumptions involving time passage are not so pressing. Solidarity and dramatization are coeval; it is not necessary to control for the events that might occur between childhood and adolescence or to defend the assumption that the boys who are being initiated are those who were exposed to certain childhood situations.

Nevertheless, the weaknesses of comparative data, even for group-level hypotheses, are marked. Comparative designs give little or no leverage on the temporal sequence of events. The use of scaling, approximations of tests of change over time, and inferences reduce—but do not eliminate—this objection. Thus the development of dramatization as solidarity increases must be left somewhat problematical. Moreover, comparisons are noticeably influenced by biases in the sample. The controls that are introduced and the use of a replication sample where feasible are only partial insurance. A third difficulty common to all precollected information is that it never contains the precise facts needed for a given index. The present investigation skirted this problem somewhat by its emphasis on formal indicators and on a topic of traditional interest, but the problem is clearly apparent in Chapter 4, for example, where an attempt is made to find direct indicators of the symbolism of male solidarity.

Testing Hypotheses in a Nonrandom Sample— Strategy of the Research

How can one judge the scientific acceptability of a cross-cultural result? The fact that most cross-cultural samples are not drawn randomly from a parent universe bars anthropology from participating in the grand strategy of other social sciences as they attempt to randomize uncontrolled factors, apply statistical tests of significance, and compare across samples. Even if comparativists were to agree to sample randomly from some arbitrarily delimited universe like Murdock's World Ethnographic Sample, the high case loss entailed by inadequate data would seriously impair the strategy.

The possibility of studying the whole universe, after the manner of the U.S. census, is also unsatisfactory. The unevenness of the data restricts the sample to well-studied societies. Compared to the enormous work involved in finding all the material that is adequate for a given problem, it might be just as well to work with fewer cases so that the problem could at least be studied more intensively. Much the same criticism applies to attempts to study the universe of a particular custom, such as Omaha kinship systems or even male initiation ceremonies. Additionally, in order to find a control group, one is forced to draw a sample from an unknown or inadequate universe.

The sample on which this report is based is similar to most cross-cultural samples in being nonrandom. Therefore, tests of significance are inappropriate. Is there then any alternative to simply reporting the results and waiting for another investigator to replicate them on another nonrandom sample? Although our answer is negative, we hope to show that analysis based on nonrandom replication is not without strength.

The strategy of random sampling and tests of significance places the emphasis on rejecting the hypothesis of no difference. After that it is an inference, and sometimes a long one, to the assertion that the investigator's particular substantive hypothesis is the correct explanation. Why not place the emphasis on comparing the hypotheses thought to be true? The method of cross-tabulating attributes that

Lazarsfeld (1955:115-25) and his associates have proposed does just this.[10] In brief, it involves the analysis of an association (and sometimes nonassociation) between two variables by using a third. The leverage given by the cross-tabulation of the third variable uncovers relationships among the initial proportions which help one to judge spuriousness, conditional factors, and causality. Sequences of relationships can be exhibited that provide much more adequate evidence for assessing a given explanation. Then if the hypothesis is applied to different units and social contexts, it emerges, if at all, as a generally adequate and well-edited conceptual map.

Thus, the strategy of this research may be outlined as follows:

a. Using a nonrandom sample, the solidarity hypothesis is tested in the empirical context of men's groups and male initiation.

b. The hypothesis is extended to females and tested in a changed context, which effectively introduces another sample.

c. The hypothesis is tested again in the still different context of corporate families and the dramatization of the parental role.

d. Using the HRAF auxiliary subsample of male initiation ceremonies, various relationships for which the original sample provided relatively few cases are replicated.

e. The three instances of the solidarity hypothesis are related to antecedent conditions so that a sequence is exhibited beginning with the community's adaptation to the physical and wider social environment, moving through the internal organization of solidarity within the community, and ending with the ritual expression and reaffirmation of this solidarity by way of dramatization.

By this kind of multivariate analysis in differing social contexts, we propose to show that the hypothesis holds despite the varied empirical challenges put to it. While anthropologists may never be confident that their generalizations are true for the universe of human societies, intensive analysis in limited samples may nonetheless uncover generalizations valid in a far broader context than that from which they were derived.

[10] See also Hyman (1955:242ff.) and Selvin (1957:519-27). Selvin's arguments on this point have been disputed by his fellow sociologists, but they seem to hold all the more for cross-cultural research.

Summary

This chapter presents an extended methodological discussion—first, because cross-cultural studies are not yet standardized and involve many pitfalls, but also because the strategy of demonstration that guided this research departs from the procedures of random sampling and statistical inference. While these procedures are appropriate for other social science problems, they are not applicable to cross-cultural comparisons.

The study sample is properly one of communities and is so treated. Only data from a particular locality group and time era were coded. The sample is not a random one, nor is it representative of any universe. Analysis shows that in comparison with the World Ethnographic Sample it is biased in favor of more modernized communities. In comparison with the societies of the Human Relations Area Files that have male initiation ceremonies, it includes more "thin," or less institutionalized, communities. There is also evidence that it is biased in favor of African and Insular Pacific areas, where male initiation rites are more frequent. However, the biases can be made to work for the investigation, and the concentration of male initiation ceremonies in two continental areas becomes an important fact to be explained.

The general strategy of hypothesis-testing in this study is of necessity one of multivariate analysis in the different social contexts permitted by the sample. Even more than other methods, this one entails replication on other samples before confidence is justified.

4. Male Solidarity and the Dramatization of Sex Role

The definition of solidarity as the cooperation of individuals in projecting a particular definition of their situation stresses a type of consensus that may come about even when the members of a group play different roles. Despite specialization—or because of it—the "team" activity converges on a kind of communication that is conveyed to some audience. The analogy with a stage production in which the lines of different characters interweave to communicate a unified impression is a correct one. In real life the range of variation of solidarity is wider, beginning with the transient impression conveyed by a group of, let us say, drunken sailors on leave to the seemingly eternal presence of an ecumenical church that comes to be called the "rock of ages." Among male groups the communications vary from the masculine claim of our society that it is proper to use rougher language and to have more personal freedom than women to the interlocking and strictly sanctioned rituals and war practices maintained by some South Sea island groups.

Someday it may be possible to measure directly the complexity and stability of these shared interpretations of the world, but the present study is restricted—in part for operational reasons—to those aspects of male culture that have been given concrete organizational form and in which all adult males of a community participate. Thus, the solidarity of male subgroups such as lodges, modern armies, unions, or fishing parties is excluded, as are also its noninstitutionalized aspects such as games, drinking patterns, sex habits, mobility, verbal expressions, differentiation of occupational role, dress, and so forth.

The solidarity concept has analogues in the work of other social scientists. In some respects it compares to a homogeneity conception of organization. Durkheim's idea of mechanical solidarity or the simpler versions of consensus (such as agreement) and modal personality may be subsumed here. Anthony Wallace (1961a:26) has recently characterized this point of view as the "replication of uniformity." Another variation is the concept of cohesion in its numerous forms of high interaction, in-group mutuality, high morale, or central values. Often this concept appears simply in its operational form, as in the sociometric indices of some small-group research. A third line of thought uses terms like "corporateness," "autonomy," or "sovereignty" and stresses the boundary-maintaining or decision-making aspect of organization.

The correspondences among these concepts need no extended analysis. Perhaps one comparison to the solidarity definition may be allowed to stand for the many others that might be made. Recently Guy E. Swanson (1960) has successfully used the sovereignty concept to illuminate the varieties of religion. He considers organizations sovereign "if they exercise original and independent jurisdiction over some sphere of social life" (1960:42). Specifically, the group must have regular communication, customary decision-making procedures, legitimacy, importance, and autonomy in the sense of not being an agency of another organization. By this definition the family and community are always sovereign, and other organizations such as chiefdoms, lineages, or clans may qualify. Although institutionalized male solidarity is not mentioned as a possibility, it seems to meet the specifications. Had Swanson been interested in the degree of sovereignty rather than in the complexity of social structure arising out of the number and combinations of such autonomous groups, the similarity to the solidarity concept would be even more apparent.

A Measure of Male Solidarity

Initial results of this study indicated that a crucial threshold of solidarity develops when all the adult males are expected to participate in an activity that has stabilized to the point of maintaining barriers to outside perception, either in the form of a building or by way of taboos against outsiders. In Goffman's terms the team has an institutionalized backstage. However, this definition does not exclude those instances where essentially the same male activity is reduplicated as an adaptation to a large population, a scattered settlement pattern, or the cross-cutting of other structures such as lineages or age grades.

Concretely then, if a community has one or more sweat houses, men's clubs, age groups, military societies, secret societies, or totemic groups and these meet the basic criteria of generality and boundedness, the men are considered solidary. Examples of nonsolidary activity by this definition are the regular card games of a portion of the Mixtec men or the age-grade villages of the Nyakyusa, which by the time they reach the point of being solidary are no longer a part of the original village.

More difficult decisions arise when solidarity is either declining or differentiating. In Ontong Java the four men's houses "have long since tumbled into ruins," and the evidence of continued exclusive male activity is questionable. However, it seemed preferable to code solidarity as present rather than make a deviant case—minimal dramatization is present—out of what was clearly a positive one in an earlier period. Another variation of minimal solidarity occurs among the Tiv, who in each homestead maintain a male "guesthouse," which is not used for other purposes. This was coded present, but the Malaita situation, where the men congregate on the front porch of the husband's house (wives have their own), was coded absent.

The Dahomeans exemplify the upper range of male solidarity, where differentiation has almost eroded the comparability of the men's groups. The Dahomeans have three types of associations: religious groups from Nigeria, coastal secret societies, and indigenous mutual-aid societies called *gbĕ*. The first two types are disqualified because they appear not to be general and women are allowed as onlookers. The *gbĕ*, in contrast, include only a few women for sexual purposes. This practice is only superficially inconsistent with the rule that the groups be exclusively male. If women may observe male activity, it reflects a permeability of the boundaries, even more than is true of saloons and snooker parlors with their swinging doors and mazelike entrances. But if a few women are the object of sexual practices or serve as mascots the way fraternity sweethearts seem to, the group is more likely to be solidary in the highest degree. The *gbě* of Dahomey are usually composed of boys who have grown up together in a particular place; there are many such groups in the community, but it is not clear whether every male feels he should join one. At the date of the ethnographic study—1931—it seems warranted to consider the men of Dahomey as solidary, but it is equally clear that they would not remain so for long.

Another example of the upper limit of solidarity is Silwa in Egypt, where only the men enter the mosque. One may speculate that in this case the size problem—Silwa has a population of 3,500—has been overcome by central organization and a higher level of abstraction of the beliefs rather than by the segmentalization that occurs in other large communities. Of course the abstraction solution has its own kind of erosion. As modernization brings secular attitudes, some adherents will cease to believe. If this decline of commitment leaves a vacuum that other religious groups attempt to fill, the outcome is very much the same as with diversification of small male groups, except that religious instead of interest differentiation predominates. The fact that only one case of centralization with abstraction of belief occurred in this sample as compared to seven cases of reduplication suggests that the latter is the more ready solution. Unfortunately, the sample contained too few cases for differential analysis.

Most of the 22 communities with male solidarity had what the ethnographers label men's houses or secret societies. Age-grading of the whole male community occurred in four societies, while military societies, sweat houses, men's houses within a compound, and exclusive attendance at the mosque occurred once each. As expected, analysis revealed no predictive utility for these content categories. The particular labels are *ad hoc* ethnographic designations that are insensitive to what appear to be the crucial variables of solidarity.

What then are the indicators of degrees of solidarity? It was hypothesized that the second step in the institutionalization process should be reflected in religious rituals. If the activities of the group have been given a religious interpretation, they tend to be more stable and easily communicated. That is, the stereotyped ritualization and dogmatization of the male activity stabilize the form of the communication and thereby insure that the meaning for the men and for the audience of women and uninitiated boys will remain the same. A third step in elaboration is reflected in a definite ranking within the organization. The status degrees of many totemic groups provide an example, but other definite deference patterns of symbols or rank were also coded. The general deference patterns based on wealth or prestige that operate in the wider community do not qualify. The rationale of this indicator is that a hierarchy of ranking reflects an elaborate, coordinated pattern of role differentiation that comes to focus on a leader or high status group. The fourth step, training or preparation for war, requires even more coordination and discipline among the men.

These items did not scale as precisely as hypothesized, but they can nonetheless be interpreted as reflecting degrees of solidarity. The percentages of the sample communities that each step cuts off are given in Table 9.

TABLE **9.**   **Index of Male Solidarity**

Step number	Item content	Per cent of sample communities
0	Informal solidarity that does not attain the generality or behavioral expression specified in step 1	59
1	Exclusive male activity participated in by all adult males and protected by physical or normative perception barriers	4
2	Ritualization of male activity, at least in part	9
3	Definite ranking of men within the activity	19
4	Training or planning for war a part of activity	9
	Total cases	(54)

Step 0 of the index was, of course, not explicitly coded and therefore does not have the same status as the others. A variety of non-institutionalized items such as individual insignia (tattooing, etc.), characteristics of men's work, attitudes toward the other sex, competitive games, etc., were tried as items without success, chiefly because they could not be coded reliably.

It was the difficulty with steps 1 and 2 that barred the index from even quasi-scale status. As the proportion (four per cent) shows, step 1, the threshold item, occurs by itself in only two communities, the

Tiv and the Fijians. On the other hand, step 2, religious ritualization, has two errors, which occur in the Thonga and Chagga cases. Even though these are the only two errors in the scale, they undermine its empirical basis because this item cuts off only two communities to begin with. Therefore, our use of these items as a sequence has only a pragmatic justification, although close consideration may persuade the reader that the advantages outweigh the disadvantages.

The alternative is to withdraw item 2 and treat the remainder as a typology. But there is much to be gained by including the ritual activity item. It calls attention to the fact that a great many of these male groups do have religious activity, even in the conventional observation categories typically used by ethnographers. One is prompted to ask whether the Thonga and Chagga male groups have rituals that were not noticed by either the ethnographer or the coders. Both these societies have community-wide age-grading, the rituals of which tend generally to be less "religious" than in other kinds of male organization. Similarly, we may wonder whether the Tiv and the Fijians do not have religious activity, but here there is more room for doubt. The very minimal and quite secular male activity of the Tiv has already been described, and the Fijian men's house also appears secularized.

These two cases could be handled by changing the cutting point and admitting only men's groups that have developed ritual activity, but we then exclude a very interesting marginal class of male activity —comparable to the village pub or some long-standing poker games— that has influence and deserves explicit consideration. Moreover, two such marginal cases also turned up in the auxiliary sample, and there was only one error in the religious activity item; this suggests that these steps, although weak, are fairly stable. Consequently, the index is presented with four steps. Its operational utility and heuristic value in later theoretical discussion seem to justify this course, and the weakness is avoided in practice by collapsing steps 1 and 2 and also steps 3 and 4.

A number of other aspects of institutionalized men's groups were tried with some success, although they did not fit the index. One of these, "informal access to nonwives" (adultery, permitted license, or tacitly approved prostitution), was coded on the 25 cases of the auxiliary sample. Societies with a high degree of solidarity (steps 3 and 4) did in fact allow such sexual contact more frequently than those with less solidarity. This was true also of another item, "religious paraphernalia on display when the men meet." Unfortunately the operational meanings of both "paraphernalia" and "display" turned out to have considerable variation. The rationale of this item is, of course, that religious "sign-vehicles" reflect greater organization of the meaning of the situation. The same interpretation can be put on a mascot or prostitute that serves the group, but this item is less frequent (one or two cases in both the study and auxiliary samples) than its prominent mention in the literature would suggest.

Other Forms of Male Solidarity

Male cooperation takes other forms than village-focused institutionalized activity. In certain types of subsistence activities and in armed conflict the same purposive coordination occurs that is the essence of solidarity, as defined in this study. Initial tests indicated that only those subsistence tasks in which all or almost all the men participated operated as alternative forms of solidarity. Specifically, these were exclusive male collective hunting, as in the driving method; fishing by driving or some forms of seining; and herding. Actually, most herding is not done collectively, but the nature of the work facilitates general communication; and modern communities, in which only a few families have herds, were excluded. To omit herding would be to ignore an important functional equivalent.

Table 10 shows that these collective male subsistence activities do in fact relate to degrees of male solidarity, as defined by the index of intravillage activities. Collective subsistence activity is assumed to determine intravillage solidarity, and the table is percentaged accordingly. Essentially the same relationship holds when herding is examined alone. However, the coding process uncovered differences in the forms of collective hunting. Some communities do it more as a sport or a celebration than as a serious food quest. The same is true of cattle herding, which in some tribes is much more than a means of livelihood. Could it be, then, that the direction of causality is, in part, the reverse? The figures support this hypothesis equally well. Perhaps the real relationship is circular: collective subsistence work leads to the institutionalization of intravillage male activity, and that in turn stimulates more collective subsistence activity, even when it

TABLE 10.   **Degree of Male Solidarity by Presence or Absence of Collective Hunting or Fishing, or of Herding**

| | COLLECTIVE HUNTING OR FISHING, OR HERDING | |
	Present	*Absent*
Noninstitutionalized male solidarity (step 0)	48	74
Institutionalized male solidarity (steps 1-2)	13	13
Highly institutionalized male solidarity (steps 3-4)	39	13
Total cases	(31)	(23)

ceases to be economically necessary. Unfortunately, the format of cross-tabulations tends to obscure such circular relationships, but they may exist just the same.

Much the same reasoning guided the investigation of warfare as a form of solidarity. The initial analysis corroborated the hypothesis that it is the forms of armed conflict that, as a unit, actively involve all or nearly all the men of the community that are associated with solidarity. Individual or family feuds or modern warfare, which draws armies from many communities, thereby breaking up the local solidarity, tend not to be associated. Local warfare that had occurred within the remembered past was expected to operate as a weaker predictor, and Table 11 demonstrates that it does.

TABLE 11.   **Degree of Male Solidarity by Type of Warfare**

	Present local warfare	*Past local warfare*	*Individual conflicts or modern armies*
Noninstitutionalized male solidarity (step 0)	42	53	72
Institutionalized male solidarity (steps 1-2)	8	29	4
Highly institutionalized male solidarity (steps 3-4)	50	18	24
Total cases	(12)	(17)	(25)

The basic pattern is similar to that found for collective subsistence work: local warfare predicts in some measure the highly institution-alized types of male solidarity, and if community conflict is absent solidarity is also likely to be absent. The latter statement is not true in six cases (comprising the deviant 24 per cent). But it seems likely that three of these (Egyptians, Dahomeans, and Thongans) preserve more of the community-based male solidarity in their supracom-munity armies than the Japanese or French do in their bureaucratic-ally organized units. One other case (the Ooldea of Australia) could be a coding error, since the Ooldea probably gave up their aboriginal warfare only a few years before they were studied. The Balinese and the Cagaba are unexplained.

The 42 per cent that should have solidarity, but do not, remind us that organized conflict is not interchangeable with intravillage male solidarity; the same is true of collective subsistence activity. There may be a simple explanation for this fact, however. By their very nature, the two extravillage forms cannot be as regular or as localized as the organization of the men within the settlement area. Thus, intracommunity solidarity may develop only when other factors allow the community to "settle down." Said another way, warfare and col-lective subsistence work may sometimes be associated with so much mobility in the community that other kinds of men's groups do not form.

The Symbolism of Male Solidarity

The exclusive activity of the males is always symbolic in the sense that it uses the conventional symbols of language or religion to express the importance of the group. Similarly, the presence of the men's house or a sacred totemic area is a constant reminder of male soli-darity. Still further removed from the activity itself are various taboos and requirements—such as the separation of men and women while eating or at the birth of a child, brother-sister avoidance, or taboos separating men from a menstruating woman—which one might ex-pect to be associated with male solidarity. Somewhat surprisingly, however, these practices are not so related, probably because they operate, as a later section will show, at the level of familial relations.

What then of the classic symbols of male power, such as the bull-roarer or masks or representations of the phallus itself? Robert Murphy (1959:96) has stated the hypothesis that guided this part of the investigation. He suggests that the integration of universally available symbolism, such as sexual symbols, into particular cultural systems is a function of social structure, particularly of the organization that is based on sex solidarity. According to Murphy, whatever may be the psychological basis of the many symbols that Freud associated with the male sex role, they are not activated unless an organized group can make use of them, so to speak, in defining its outlook on the world. If this hypothesis is true, such symbolism should be found more frequently when male solidarity is highly institutionalized.

Unfortunately, there is a serious problem of operationalization. It begs the question to look for "male symbols," and a check list tends to have infinite variations. As a consequence, this study did not find a reliable classification independent of the masculinity principle. Nonetheless, one tentative result based on the auxiliary sample is reported here because it is suggestive. The coders simply looked for objects which, even in the absence of men, signify to the women and children of the community the presence of male activity or strong male influence. Masks have this significance fairly frequently, as do bull-roarers, drums, and spears. Trophies of war, such as shrunken heads, special insignia, or headgear, were also allowed. A majority of the 22 communities with male solidarity have such symbolism, and the proportion increases regularly with each step of the solidarity index. All but one of the seven communities with the highest degree of institutional elaboration (step 4) have such public symbols.

The difficulty with the hypothesis that male solidarity heightens the salience of individually available symbols is not that it does not fit the facts, which it appears to do, but that it does not sufficiently deepen our knowledge of these facts. The central question in terms of the dramaturgical framework is that of the functions these symbols fulfill. The problem is especially interesting when we consider the paradox that although many of these symbols are forbidden to the uninitiated, sometimes on pain of death, there is much evidence that the women and young boys know very well that bull-roarers make the whirring sound that "frightens" them or that their fathers or brothers are dressed up as masked spirits. In his sensitive treatment of men and masks among the Lakalai of New Britain, Valentine remarks on this point:

> All the supplementary mystification which surrounds the masks and the performances not only contributes to masculine pride but heightens the atmosphere of secrecy and the sense of the uncanny as well. Sanctity and taboo further intensify these effects. None but the initiated may handle the masks or witness the transformations from ordinary person to masked man.
>
> Yet virtually the only real secrets beneath all this elaborate cultural camouflage are the details of the internal structures of the masks and the procedures surrounding their construction [1961:48].

What then is the point of it all? We are forced to conclude that the crucial aspect of this interplay is simply that people should participate, that the women should play the men's game, keeping their distance and expressing awe and fear, while the men, when they wear the costume, demonstrate to their fellows that they are loyal and disciplined in this setting. The symbol merely provides a focus for these social exercises; after all, one cannot show that one can keep a secret unless there is some secret to keep, nor can one be expected to be impressed unless there is at least an attempt at impressiveness. The ultimate function of these symbols, in this view, is to reinforce the delicate social control maintained in human communities by providing a kind of "practice bar" for social forms.

Male Initiation Ceremonies in Relation to Solidarity

What happens when a new member is taken into this complex structure of coordinated interaction and belief that is summed up in the term solidarity? What can be done, so to speak, to preserve the surface tension of cultural meanings that the men have elaborated? All groups face this threat when members enter or leave or when there is an internal shift of status. The men must accommodate the new member as he adapts to them, but in addition, the audience—whether the women, the candidate's uninitiated peers, or the members of other communities—must be led to accept the candidate's new status and the continuation of the tissue of social meaning that existed before.

The solution to this social maintenance problem is to arrange a special dramatization of the status change, which then serves, insofar as the performers and the audience cooperate in their roles, as a practice session for the real thing—which is believing that the boy is an acceptable instance of the class of socially functional males. If the audience can be led to imagine the new situation with the help of a little staging, it will find it easier to continue doing so and will then finally be so taken in by the whole thing that it comes to accept the change as permanent, real, and legitimate. Of course, a certain amount of additional dramaturgical effort must be expended after the initiation ceremony. If the boy does not respond to the women as if he were a man, if he does not begin to hunt seriously, to feel responsibility and loyalty to the community, and to show by various shifts in habit that he conceives of himself as different, doubts may arise—not that dramatization does not always achieve its purpose, but that the boy is somehow mentally incompetent!

The use of a dramaturgical framework has a disadvantage in that the reader may think that the natives are quite conscious of the whole process, as indeed they are of parts of it. But there is no reason to believe that nonliterate people are any more or less sophisticated than those moderns who strive to become Elks, Masons, Knights of this or that, or SS men. Or, to take more comparable examples, their status shift is just as convincing and determining as are the career movements that lead urban males to think of themselves as doctors, lawyers, merchants, or chiefs.

The test of the central hypothesis is made in Table 12. It brings together the two measures of male solidarity and initiation dramatization in order to exhibit the concomitant variation that is present in the association.

It is clear that as male solidarity is more institutionalized, the elaboration of initiation ceremonies increases. The few markedly deviant cases, indicated by the low proportions, repay special examination. Four communities have some degree of solidarity but lack the expected degree of dramatization. Those with high solidarity are the Bontoc Igorot and the Egyptians; the two with low solidarity are the Navaho and the New Irelanders. On the other hand, three societies have no institutionalized solidarity but do have initiation ceremonies. These are the Jivaro, the Ojibwa, and the Azande, the last of which has elaborate initiation. The details on each are given below, including

TABLE 12. **Relationship of Degrees of Male Sex-Role Dramatization to Degrees of Male Solidarity**

	INSTITUTIONALIZATION OF MALE SOLIDARITY**		
DEGREE OF DRAMATIZATION*	*None* (*step 0*)	*Low* (*steps 1-2*)	*High* (*steps 3-4*)
Undramatic sex-role recognition (0 step)	91	14	13
Individualized dramatization (steps 1-2)	6	72	33
Group dramatization (steps 3-4)	3	14	54
Total cases	(32)	(7)	(15)

* For scale, see Table 1, p. 15.
** For scale, see Table 9, p. 67.

their exact level on each scale, from 0 to 4, with the solidarity index given first.

Bontoc Igorot (4, 0): The ethnographer Jenks explicitly denies the presence of an initiation ceremony in this solidary community: "No notice whatever is taken of it by the social group. This nonobservance of the fact of puberty would be very remarkable ... were it not for the fact that the Igorot has developed the *olag*—an institution [a young people's clubhouse] calculated to emphasize the fact and significance of puberty" (1905:66). He also mentions that most boys are circumcised between the ages of four and seven, but without any attendant ceremony.

Egyptians (3, 0): Exclusive male attendance at the mosque is an unusual form of solidarity, but it fits the conceptual definition and was therefore coded present. There is no evidence of an adolescent ceremony, although boys between the ages of three and six are circumcised and experience an elaborate ceremony that is identical in form with those held in other places. One may speculate that dramatization at an earlier age is a kind of degeneration of the ceremony, but there is no direct evidence to support this view.

Navaho (2, 0): Each homestead has its sweat house, which at the time of the study retained some religious overtones. In conservative areas boys wait until puberty to assume a breechcloth and to take a sweat bath alone, but to Navajo adults neither of these customs has importance, which in this study is taken as a necessary indicator of social recognition.

New Irelanders (2, 3): The relatively elaborate initiation is not matched by a highly institutionalized men's group, although the discrepancy is the sort that could result from inadequate data or imprecise coding.

Ojibwa (0, 2): The ethnographers Hilger and Densmore secured a clear-cut retrospective account of the vision quest, but the evidence for male solidarity does not justify coding it present. There is indication that sweat houses were formerly important to the men as a group, and the Midewiwin ceremony is even compared to a Masonic lodge meeting, but it is not clear that all village men participated in the ceremony.

Jivaro (0, 2): The description of initiation is clear, but the only indication of male solidarity is the division of the houses into a men's and a women's side.

Azande (0, 3): This group has secret societies, but they are mostly bisexual. Each homestead has a husband's hut, separate from those of the wives, but this is below the acceptable level of institutionalization.

The deviant-case analysis prompts a further consideration. The indication of inadequate data and insensitive coding in the relatively few deviant cases seems to rule out the possibility that another major variable is operative. Indeed, the association is so strong as to raise the question of a unitary phenomenon of which the two variables are simply parts. Such a unitary pattern could not be simply that initiation rites are the entrance requirements of formal organizations. The finding in Chapter 1 that many ceremonies are in no way related to the operation of a formal organization, if it exists in the community at all, negates this possibility. If the phenomenon is described as a community-wide structure of shared orientation among males that includes the interpretation of a new member's status, then the unitary character of the two variables is plausible. But that is essentially what the solidarity hypothesis asserts. If the association of solidarity and dramatization now seems so close that it is belittled as a tautology or "simple common sense," it is a credit more to the theory from which it derives than to the inherent simplicity of the relationship.

A Test of a Psychogenic Hypothesis

Standing in sharp contrast to the solidarity hypothesis is Whiting's psychogenic explanation, which emphasizes sex-role conflict as the key causal factor leading to initiation ceremonies. Previous chapters have taken up both the theory and the general methodology of this interpretation; it remains to test the association when male solidarity is controlled.

As an empirical indicator of female sex-role identification Whiting uses the presence of an exclusive mother-son sleeping arrangement. This item was coded in the present study with some difficulty because in many cases the information was simply not present. It is for this reason that ten cases have been omitted from Table 13, which summarizes the test. Whiting was able to code these cases only by using substitute information (1962:391 ff.). If the society had polygyny and separate mother-child households, and if the husband rotated among his wives so that he was absent from his nursing wife's hut at least 50 per cent of the time, Whiting assumed the presence of an exclusive mother-son sleeping arrangement. Such a substitution may be legitimate from one point of view, but it is wholly unjustified if one is really trying to test the predictive efficiency of this childhood experience and not the indirect effect of a large structural pattern. It so happens that the cluster of items is strongly associated with male solidarity, so Whiting has in effect introduced the latter variable unwittingly. Whiting's second indicator, patrilocal residence, is as Murdock coded it in the World Ethnographic Sample. As is customary, the instances of uxoripatrilocal residence are considered patrilocal.

Dramatization and male solidarity are dichotomized for this test into present and absent, with the former category including all degrees. The table is percentaged in order to show the overall pattern. Although the small number of cases does not usually justify such treatment, the statistical analysis of the raw data given below coincides with the results obtained by inspection.

With all the drawbacks of this table, it is apparent that male solidarity dissolves the relationship between the two childhood factors and male initiation. In the crucial cells, where solidarity is present but the two childhood factors are absent, and the reverse of

TABLE 13. **Dramatization of Male Sex Role by Exclusive Mother-Son Sleeping Arrangement and Patrilocal Residence When Male Solidarity Is Controlled**

	Exclusive sleeping arrangement	Patrilocal residence	Male sex-role dramatization		Total cases
			Present	Absent	
Male solidarity present	+	+	86	14	(7)
	+	−	100	0	(4)
	−	+	83	17	(6)
	−	−	67	33	(3)
Total cases			(17)	(3)	
Male solidarity absent	+	+	33	67	(3)
	+	−	0	100	(2)
	−	+	7	93	(13)
	−	−	0	100	(6)
Total cases			(2)	(22)	

this, the psychogenic hypothesis fails. Admittedly, the number of cases in the cells is small, but this shortage merely emphasizes the fact that the solidarity hypothesis predicts more parsimoniously than the combination of variables required for the role-conflict explanation.

But if these individual-level factors do not operate independently, could they then be part of a developmental sequence? This is of course a possibility, but in this case it seems more reasonable to interpret these factors as completely spurious in the sense that they are adventitious. The bias that was built into the exclusive sleeping arrangement factor when it was coded on the basis of substitute data has already been cited. Aside from that bias, it now seems that the sleeping arrangement of mother and son is simply an artifact of the social structure and does not result in any lasting psychological tendencies in either the boy or the mother—nor in any infant girls, who seem always to be ignored in Whiting's hypotheses even though they are exposed to the same situations. Similarly, male envy and subsequent identification may not be imputed to patrilocal residence. Insofar as these two factors have any predictive power at all, it is because they indirectly reflect male solidarity. In combination they tap the cluster of structural factors that is highly associated with male organization.

Since both hypotheses use the same sample, it is possible to compare the relative efficiency by computing Goodman and Kruskal's coefficient of predictability.[1] These are .74 and .32 respectively for the solidarity and the sex-role conflict hypotheses.

A *Laboratory Experiment Relating Initiation Ceremonies and Solidarity*

The essential relationship proposed in this study has been supported, quite independently, by a laboratory experiment contrived by Elliot Aronson and Judson Mills (1959:177-81). They set out to test the hypothesis that persons who undergo an unpleasant initiation to become members of a group come to view the group more favorably. If we assume that many favorable appraisals of the group activity and membership is a measure of what has been here defined as solidarity, then the experiment may be taken as evidence in support of the link between such a property of the group and the special entrance experiences of initiation. They describe the experiment as follows:

> College women who volunteered to participate in discussion groups were randomly assigned to one of three experimental conditions: A *Severe* initiation condition, a *Mild* initiation condition, and a *Control* condition. In the Severe condition, subjects were required to read some embarrassing material before joining the group; in the Mild condition the material they read in order to join the group was not very embarrassing; in the Control condition, subjects were not required to read any material before becoming group members. Each subject listened to a recording that appeared to be an ongoing discussion being conducted by the group which she had just joined. Afterwards, subjects filled out a questionnaire evaluating the discussion and the participants. The results clearly verified the hypothesis. The subjects who underwent a Severe initiation perceived the group as being significantly more attractive than did those who underwent a Mild initiation or no initiation. There was no appreciable difference between ratings by subjects who underwent a Mild initiation and those by subjects who underwent no initiation [1959:181].

[1] A brief explanation of this measure may be found in Zelditch (1959:178ff.).

Aronson and Mills interpret their results in terms of Festinger's theory of cognitive dissonance. The unpleasant initiation experience is dissonant with believing the group is ordinary, so compensation in the form of a favorable evaluation of the group is required for group membership to be worth the original annoyance. Of course, as soon as the results of the experiment are interpreted in these pleasure–pain terms so dear to hearts of psychologists, the experiment ceases to be a test of a general phenomenon. The fact is that most initiations cannot legitimately be considered unpleasant. Only a portion of initiation ceremonies around the world would fit this pattern. Indeed, the evidence presented in Chapter 1 suggests that even for those ceremonies that are objectively painful, the experience may not be the significant social meaning. In this particular experiment it is a matter of interpretation whether or not reading "embarrassing material" in the form of vivid descriptions of sexual activity from contemporary novels is unpleasant. The experimenters report that only one of 43 girls declined to take the test, so the experience was obviously not unpleasant in the sense of being repellent.

If the results of the experiment admit of no interpretation other than overevaluation of the group to compensate for the unpleasant initiation, then it conflicts with the interpretation proposed for the cross-cultural results. But there may be a more general way of stating both the dramatization and dissonance explanations. If it assumed that the embarrassment of the experimental initiation is, fundamentally, a means of making the stimulus clear, so that a definite conception of future group activity is formed in the mind of the candidate, then we may interpret the subsequent favorable appraisal of the group as an alignment of new data with the initial frame of reference. The appraisal will be favorable or unfavorable depending upon the direction given in the initiation; in the present case, there is good reason to believe that the basic set toward the experience was favorable, despite the "embarrassment" and the boring character of the group discussion. This more general interpretation is still quite close to the dramaturgical framework, but it extends it by suggesting the kind of psychological mechanism that might operate. As for the experiment, a further test is suggested that controls on the pleasant-unpleasant assumption by using a pleasant initiation as the independent variable.

Needless to say, the acceptance of this experiment as support for the solidarity hypothesis does not exclude the possibility that Whiting's hypothesis, with its child-training determinants, still holds. The two are not mutually incompatible, although an experiment dealing with Whiting's factors would be desirable. A second point is that the direction of causality in the experiment is superficially the reverse of that asserted in the solidarity hypothesis. But the difference is mainly one of point of view and unit of analysis. The experiment uses individuals as the unit, while the cross-cultural study focuses on the group. Furthermore, the phrasing of the solidarity hypothesis in terms of the functional paradigm permits, and indeed requires, both directions, or circularity, of causation.

Associated Ceremonies of Growing Up

If customs such as exclusive mother-son sleeping arrangements and patrilocality show some association with male solidarity and initiation, then the prior question must be answered of the relationship of these two central variables to customs more closely related conceptually— that is, to other rites attendant on growing up.

Besides the clusters of ritual practices that define initiation ceremonies and those surrounding birth, there are three other types of customs that a boy may experience as he grows up. During adolescence he may shift his sleeping quarters from the domestic establishment to the men's house, to a bachelor's hut or sleeping area, to the house of a kinsman, or simply to a place removed from the sleeping area of his parents. Although the coding did not distinguish between these variations, 28 of the 54 sample societies had some such custom for boys. In only six societies was there some change in girls' sleeping quarters. These six societies also had a male shift, making 21 per cent of the societies with this custom that apply it to both sexes. In comparison, of the 35 sample societies with initiation for one or the other of the sexes, 49 per cent have it for both.

A second type of practice occurs at about five to eight years of age and will be called boyhood ceremonies. Of the 15 communities with either male or female ceremonies of this preadolescent type, 12 have them for both sexes. In general the coders looked for the same kinds of customs previously noted for initiation, but the requirement that adults be present was relaxed. Thus, tooth filing, tattooing, and other youthful decoration practices were checked, as were family ceremonies, ritual introduction to work, or circumcision at this early age. The presence of boyhood ceremonies in the three societies (Bontoc Igorot, Egyptians, and Navaho) with male solidarity but no initiation suggests that had the coders been instructed to accept for study the most elaborate male ceremony regardless of the age of the boys, there would have been no deviant cases. Unfortunately, the coding rules were not sufficiently refined at the outset.

The third type occurs at about two or three years of age. A boy may be given his first haircut, or have his ears pierced, or be given gifts in recognition of his first steps or words. The diversity of the occasion suggests that the function of the ceremony is something other than recognition of a boy's new ability. Rather, he provides more of an excuse for a family occasion. Of the ten societies with these childhood ceremonies, nine apply them to both sexes.

These basic facts bear on questions that naturally arise in the analysis of sex-role dramatization. The general frequency of these rituals in relation to initiation and the proportion of the sample having such customs for both sexes, although on separate occasions, have been discussed. But how is the presence of these other ceremonies associated with initiation rites? Specifically, are they typically associated, acting as supplements, or are they functional alternatives, occurring when there is solidarity but no initiation?

Table 14 shows the association of male sex-role dramatization with these three types of customs.

The trend of the percentages in each column reflects the previously noted fact that the customs have different frequencies, at least in this sample. The difference between the proportions indicates an association with dramatization in the case of adolescent shift of sleeping quarters and boyhood ceremonies, but no such association for childhood festivities. If the notion of functional equivalence is given a strict interpretation as an either/or phenomenon, then none of these customs is such an equivalent because each overlaps to some extent with initiation ceremonies. If a more restricted definition of functional equivalence is used and we ask whether alternative customs appear when solidarity exists without initiation, then the answer is that in the

TABLE 14. Association of Male Sex-Role Dramatization with Three Other Customs of Growing Up: Shift of Adolescents' Sleeping Quarters, Ceremonies of Boyhood, and Ceremonies of Childhood

| | MALE SEX-ROLE DRAMATIZATION AT ADOLESCENCE | |
	Present	*Absent*
Shift of adolescents' sleeping quarters	64	44
Total cases	(22)	(32)
Boyhood ceremony	36	20
Total cases	(22)	(30)
Childhood ceremony	18	20
Total cases	(22)	(30)

three cases available (Bontoc Igorot, Egyptians, and Navaho) all have boyhood ceremonies and shift of sleeping quarters, but only one has a childhood ritual. So in this sense two of the customs do operate as alternatives. But the interpretation rests on only three cases, and it is further attenuated when one recalls that initiation ceremonies can be more rigorously defined so that age is disregarded. If that is done, three of the boyhood ceremonies become initiation rites and there are no deviant cases of this type.

Perhaps a more fruitful observation is that childhood ceremonies which tend not to distinguish sex are not associated with male initiation ceremonies. They seem to be of another class, not part of any growing-up sequence that culminates in initiation. Just the opposite is true of boyhood ceremonies which are strongly associated with male solidarity as well as with male initiation. Shift of sleeping quarters, while as strongly related to initiation ceremonies, is less strongly related to solidarity, but the diversity of customs that were accepted for this category rules out any but a superficial interpretation.

In order to make sense out of the occurrence of these customs, it is necessary to jump ahead of the story a bit. Later analysis will suggest that initiation and male solidarity both reflect the level of community organization; childhood ceremonies, like the couvade, relate to family structure. Shift of sleeping quarters seems to overlap the two levels.

These hypotheses are oversimplified, but they embody the distinction between community and family units that becomes increasingly important in the course of the analysis.

Summary

It is possible to measure male solidarity by a four-step index that reflects increasing coordination of the men in defining their role and objectives. In addition to the defining item of boundary maintenance, these steps include religious activity, ranking, and preparation for war. While all societies have some male solidarity, these steps define the institutionalization of male activity on a community-wide basis. Degrees of solidarity, as measured by this index, are associated with the presence of collective, exclusively male subsistence activity and with warfare of a local or intercommunity type.

Male solidarity relates even more strongly to degrees of dramatization of the male sex role, which is the central result of the study.

Other customs of growing up are analyzed in relation to dramatization, to yield the finding that preadolescent ceremonies and a shift of sleeping quarters at adolescence—but not ceremonies for boys during childhood—are associated with male initiation ceremonies.

5. The Preconditions of Solidarity

The antecedent conditions of institutionalized male cohesion may be classified according to the type of system that they reflect. Thus, it is conceivable that the gene pool of the human group may, in certain of its combinations, influence the tendency of the men to band together. Another, somewhat similar type of system is the aggregate of personalities: temperament, predominant defense reactions, or modally held attitudes may operate as preconditions of male solidarity. A third class has been labeled ecological: these determinants arise out of the interaction of men with their physical and biological environment as they make a living. A fourth type, the other social systems in contact with a community, does not, of course, differ from it in the same way in which the system of plants and animals differs; but all other social systems share the potentiality of reaction to the particular community under study and thus form a separate class of environmental determinants.

Some of the reasons for setting aside genetic and personality systems have already been indicated. The study of these factors is probably not possible with present cross-cultural data, but even if it were, it is a reasonable assumption that they would operate as just so much random variation with respect to group-level hypotheses. Consequently, the emphasis of this research falls on ecological and social system influences. It is assumed that both these types of factors may systematically influence the structure of communities. The ecological system acts more sluggishly, simply because the distribution and type of plants and animals is more stable, but it is reasonable to expect nonrandom effects. Social systems, benefiting from the efficiency of symbolic communication, act more precisely and pervasively even though the pressure may not be sustained over long periods of time.

Three kinds of social groups may impinge on the interacting male organization. There is, first of all, the countergroup made up of the women and uninitiated boys. Second, the community may have transactions with other communities of approximately the same organizational level. This interaction tends to be one of male contacts, although the whole community may suffer raids or enjoy intergroup festivities. Third, the men and the whole community must often deal with systems having a markedly more complex organization. Such relationships are the type case of acculturation studies.

Intersystem influences such as these present a methodological problem that cannot be overcome with present techniques of cross-cultural analysis. Undoubtedly involved is a process of circular causality that is not revealed by correlations. For instance, it may be that an attack on a community not only increases solidarity among the defenders, but also leads to stereotype formation. Then the enemy is endowed with attributes of ferocity that it perhaps does not possess. The solidarity of the defenders may nonetheless increase to meet the threat. Similarly, hunting large animals that move in herds may bring the men into close interaction, but they may maintain this cohesion in the form of yearly rabbit drives long after the buffalo are gone or even after rabbits are required for food.

It is this assumption that prompted the interpretation in Chapter 4 of collective subsistence activity and intercommunity warfare as aspects of solidarity. However, in this chapter these and other similar factors will be looked upon as antecedent conditions. No claim is made that they are decisively causal. Perhaps the correct perspective is that "antecedent" is a matter of degree, moving from the initial responsiveness of ecological and social systems through the initial reaction of the men in given communities and then, by continued reciprocal influence, to the stable institutionalization of male cooperation that is maintained autonomously.

The Subsistence Base

Julian Steward (1955), among others, has analyzed the way in which the distribution of different types of plants and animals, in conjunction with the available technology for exploiting it, affects social structure: thus, the meager and scattered pickings available to the Paiute of California and Nevada limited their basic unit of organization to the small family, while the system of river control and irrigation of the Near Eastern civilizations led to totalitarian states. One of the important variables of his formulation appears to be the distribution of the food supply, which involves such specific factors as localization, aggregation, and yearly fluctuation. These in turn, it may be hypothesized, influence the probability that the males of a society will interact with one another to the exclusion of females. If the items of food supply are distributed in a way that permits their exploitation by two large groups working separately—that is, male and female teams— then male (and female) solidarity is facilitated. In line with this general interpretation, Murdock's ratings (1957:668) of the types of plants and animals exploited by the societies of the study sample, (supplemented by newly coded data when necessary) were combined into a typology of subsistence patterns as follows:

Food-gathering (17 per cent of the study sample) Domesticated crops or animals absent, unimportant, or recent; and food is secured by hunting, fishing, gathering, or some combination of these. This category includes many diverse types of exploitation that might be separated for other purposes or larger samples, but they are alike in the fact that subsistence is basically hand-to-mouth.

Horticulture (33 per cent) Cultivation or tending of roots, tubers, or trees, but no cereals. Any large domesticated animals must be aboriginally derived. Most of these communities are in Oceania. The term horticulture is here arbitrarily limited to noncereal crops, although technically it may apply to any crop if it is cultivated in small plots without the use of a plough.

Traditional Agriculture (35 per cent) Cultivation of some kind of cereal crop, with aboriginally derived large domesticated animals present in most cases. The herding Lapps are placed in this category because they do in fact depend upon cereal crops, which are obtained from sedentary communities.

Modern Agriculture (15 per cent) Cultivation of cereal crops and the presence of domesticated large animals introduced through European contact. Besides such obvious groups as the French, the modernized Navaho and Papago fall into this category.

Thus the typology is basically one of kind of staple crop, with the cereal cultivators further divided with respect to the use of large domestic animals that have been introduced by contact. More fundamentally, the typology attempts to tap the preconditions of the organization of subsistence work. In modern agriculture, for example, with the plough and traction animals widely available, women tend to withdraw from farm work. Moreover, in modern agriculture men do not interact regularly because their farms are usually separated.

At the other extreme, among food-gatherers, somewhat the same situation arises for different reasons. The male food-gatherers may be separated because of the scant and widely distributed food supply, and in extreme cases the women may be subject to the same scattering. However, the marginal life of food-gatherers is easily exaggerated. An equally frequent state of affairs is that the band lives in a particular territory and the animals and plants are both abundant enough and distributed compactly enough to justify collective, although sex-segregated, exploitation.

Often the ecological conditions of food-gathering are even more favorable to the separation of the sexes and of high interaction within sex groups than is true among horticulturalists, who tend to be the type case. Among the latter group, the women tend the gardens or other small plots. Often a number of them work together, and almost always they see one another at work. The crop is usually not overly abundant, and they work with digging sticks so that many female hands are required. The men help with the clearing and other heavy work, but they are typically free for hunting, war, trade, or ceremonies. Their business tends to keep them in and around the village, so that male interaction is facilitated.

The fourth type, traditional agriculture, may at times approximate the horticulture pattern. When cereals are cultivated in small plots and with crude implements, the women may be involved as before. But the men work also, and the trend is toward lesser female participation. For a time the women may be able to interact freely in the village, enjoying the same freedom that the males do in horticultural societies. But as modernization proceeds, both men and women are separated from others of their sex by the dispersal of homesteads and the increasing use of animals.

This general interpretation is tested in Table 15, which shows the association of these four subsistence types to degrees of solidarity. The trend conforms to the hypothesis in that the horticulturalists show the highest frequency of institutionalized male solidarity, an association that explains why men's clubs and initiation are so prevalent in Oceania and Africa. However, the differences are not striking; very likely the subsistence types are not sufficiently sensitive to the segregation and high interaction within sex groups that are hypothesized to be crucial. The table further indicates that traditional agriculture and food-gathering are alike in showing no minimal institutionalization of solidarity although they both have the highly institutionalized levels. The one case of male solidarity among those with modern agriculture is the Navaho. Their sweat baths appear to be a passing vestige.

TABLE 15. **Relationship of Degree of Solidarity to Subsistence Type**

	Modern agriculture	*Traditional agriculture*	*Horticulture*	*Food-gathering*
Noninstitutionalized male solidarity (step 0)	88	61	47	56
Institutionalized male solidarity (steps 1-2)	12	0	32	0
Highly institutionalized male solidarity (steps 3-4)	0	39	21	44
Total cases	(8)	(18)	(19)	(9)

If it is true that certain subsistence patterns are more conducive than others to the segregation and grouping of the sexes—a pattern of organization that may now be labeled sexual bifurcation[1]—then more direct measures of the interaction of men and women should deepen our understanding of the subsistence types. Thus, collective male subsistence activity, which was previously shown to relate to male solidarity, is differentially present in the four subsistence types, as is shown in Table 16.

The two communities that have modern agriculture and also have collective male subsistence activity are the Papago and the Navaho.

[1] I am indebted to Pauline M. Kolenda for calling my attention to this usage of W. Lloyd Warner's (1958:131).

TABLE 16. Relationship of Collective Male Subsistence Activity to Subsistence Type

	Modern agriculture	*Traditional agriculture*	*Horticulture*	*Food-gathering*
Collective male subsistence activity	25	83	53	44
Total cases	(8)	(18)	(19)	(9)

They were so classified because their herding is not yet as individualized and rationalized as it is among groups like the Homestead Texans. Herding also accounts for the high proportion of communities with traditional agriculture that were coded as having collective male subsistence activity. Among the horticulturalists and food-gatherers, collective fishing or hunting brings the men together, but it is important to note that the hunting may take many different forms within its generally collective organization.

Warfare, the other male activity that is associated with male solidarity, shows a different relationship to these subsistence types. The distribution of types of warfare is shown in Table 17, which suggests that the level at which such organized conflict is carried on rises as one moves from the food-gatherers to the modern agriculturalists. Thus, the former fight at an individual level, or else their intercommunity conflict was still going on at the time they were studied. The horticulturalists were more frequently classified as having warfare in the past, which reflects the "pacification" that has usually ensued before the ethnographer arrives. Those groups with traditional agriculture show either past local warfare or supracommunity armies: half the communities making up the 44 per cent participate in native or colonial armies. This trend is completed among the modern agriculturalists, who never fight as local communities.

Examining these two correlates of male solidarity together may yield an explanation of the fact, shown in Table 15, that the traditional agriculturalists and food-gatherers have only highly institutionalized male solidarity. The indication is that the herding of the agriculturalists and the active warfare of the hunters strongly condition the more localized forms of solidarity that may develop.

Although warfare and collective male subsistence activity seem

TABLE 17. **Relationship of Type of Warfare to Subsistence Type**

	Modern agriculture	*Traditional agriculture*	Horticulture	*Food-gathering*
Individual conflicts or supracommunity armies	100	44	26	44
Past local warfare	0	44	48	0
Present local warfare	0	12	26	56
Total cases	(8)	(18)	(19)	(9)

to operate as direct preconditions, or perhaps as alternate forms, of male solidarity, it is easy to imagine that in some communities males come together indirectly as a consequence of the organization of the women. The most obvious form of female organization would be collective subsistence activity, comparable to that of the men. But this turned out to be rare: there are only ten instances in the sample. Instead, the subsistence activity of females typically operates at the family level.

Although the ethnographic accounts are not always explicit on the matter, it seems reasonable to assume that the women in polygynous or extended family households cooperate in their work. Perhaps "coordinate" is a better word, inasmuch as the wives of one man may work for the family unit only indirectly as they take care of their own gardens and children. On this assumption the communities that Murdock coded as having general polygyny or extended families were grouped together to form a category of communities with "multi-female household organization." In one respect this is a fairly homogeneous category because most extended families are also polygynous. It is also homogeneous in another way. Murdock's code deals with modal types. Thus, a community is said to have extended families if most families are so organized. Similarly, general polygyny is considered present if 20 per cent or more of the men have more than one wife. It might be objected that this classification ignores the actual variation in the community—some men, after all, will have only one wife. But in practice this is no problem because the men with one wife usually live with their father, who may have two wives. Thus, the son's wife is often in the same work group as his father's wives.

Similar reasoning applied in justifying the combination of Murdock's lineal and stem families with his limited polygyny. The third category is that of the monogamous, independent family, that is, the typical American family. Here the interaction among women is severely limited by the fact that each household contains only one adult female.

Under what conditions are multifemale households functional? Traditionally the "dominance of women" has been ascribed to control of subsistence activity, particularly of gardens. But female dominance is probably an overinterpretation. The women may do most of the work in the gardens and may even own them, but the males typically exert considerable control. A more reasonable interpretation is that gardening, gathering, and some tasks in traditional agricultural communities require extensive manual labor. Weeding, picking berries, or digging witchety grubs is tedious work and is productive only if many hands are applied for a long time. Aside from slaves, which require a more complex social organization for their control, women have been the usual recipients of these colorless but necessary subsistence tasks. And the two patterns most often associated with the securing of such a labor force are polygynous marriages and extended families. It is of course true that extended families also provide a corps of able-bodied men, which is additionally necessary in some types of subsistence patterns, but this circumstance only contributes to the probability that sexual bifurcation will develop in such communities.

Table 18 exhibits the relationship of multifemale household organization to the four subsistence types. The horticulturalists are most likely to have such organization, followed by the traditional agriculturalists. The limited female family is predominant among the food-gatherers; this perhaps reflects the incompatibility of nomadism and an unpredictable food supply with the extended family. The single-woman family is increasingly frequent as one moves from the food-gatherers to the modern agriculturalists.

Table 19 completes the picture, within the limits of available cases, of the functioning of multifemale household organization. Like collective male subsistence activity and warfare, there is an association with male solidarity. However, the most elaborate form of this organization accounts for most of the difference. Either general polygyny and/or extended families reflect some kind of structural

TABLE 18. **Relationship of Type of Female Household Organization to Subsistence Type**

	Modern agriculture	*Traditional agriculture*	*Horticulture*	*Food-gathering*
Multifemale household organization	25	55	68	44
Limited female household organization	38	28	21	56
Monogamous independent families	37	17	11	0
Total cases	(8)	(18)	(19)	(9)

threshold, or else some factor other than the number of women is reflected in the table. Inasmuch as this family type is quite broad and includes in it a multitude of other factors—like corporate family organization, multiple men, etc.—the association might well be spurious. Only more refined investigation will tell. If there were more cases so that the instances of general polygyny and extended families could be separated, some advance might be made on this point. But the high degree of overlap precludes such differential analysis.

TABLE 19. **Degree of Male Solidarity by Type of Female Household Organization**

	Monogamous independent families	*Limited female household organization*	*Multifemale household organization*
Noninstitutionalized male solidarity (step 0)	75	82	42
Institutionalized male solidarity (steps 1-2)	13	6	17
Highly institutionalized male solidarity (steps 3-4)	12	12	41
Total cases	(8)	(17)	(29)

The foregoing discussion, tentative as it is, suggests that each subsistence type has a typical or predominant bifurcation factor. Among the traditional agriculturalists, collective male subsistence activity, especially herding, is present in 83 per cent of the cases. Among horticulturalists, multifemale household organization occurs in 68 per cent. And among the food-gatherers, active local warfare is true of 56 per cent.

How then do these factors combine with the others? If we allow multifemale household organization and village-wide collective female subsistence activity to alternate as indicators of the sexual division of labor on the women's side, and warfare and collective male subsistence activity to stand for the male side, how do the subsistence types compare? What interests us is the proportion of each type that may be considered sexually bifurcated in the above sense. The result may be easily summarized by saying that 33 per cent of the food-gatherers are bifurcated. That is, one-third of these communities have either multifemale household organization or collective female subsistence activity *and* warfare or collective male subsistence activity. Similarly, 74 per cent of the horticulturalists, 61 per cent of the traditional agriculturalists, and 12 per cent of the modern agriculturalists are bifurcated. These proportions are not out of line with the actual occurrence of male solidarity, as shown in Table 15. The simplest interpretation of these patterns is that sexual bifurcation may be built of a variety of determinants; and when it occurs, it is likely to be capped by institutionalized male solidarity.

There is one other factor—cited before—which on the surface should reflect sexual bifurcation by itself. That factor is unilocal residence. Although generally known, the hypothesis is explicitly stated by Robert Murphy:

> Related to this opposition between the sexes, there is a tendency also for men's organizations of the type under discussion to be associated with unilocal residence. Unilocality, especially when accompanied by frequent marriage outside the local group, . . . keeps consanguines of one sex together while sending those of the opposite away. Members of the opposite sex thus tend to be outsiders and affines, and the forms of opposition common to the latter relationships complement sex antagonism [1959:97].

Unfortunately, this hypothesis is more difficult to test than one would expect. As coded by Murdock, most of the societies in this sample have unilocal residence rules (including avunculocal and uxoripatrilocal). Even 75 per cent of those classified as modern agriculturalists have unilocal rules; only eight communities do not have them. The same shortage of cases applies to any attempt to test the differential influence of matrilocal and patrilocal residence. About the best one can say is that there is a tendency, which might be improved with finer coding, for modern agriculturalists, in contrast to the three other subsistence types, to lack unilocal rules of residence and male solidarity.

It would be extremely satisfying to be able to present a table that would show the interrelations between subsistence type and collective male subsistence activity, warfare, and multifemale household organization—and between all of these and male solidarity. Obviously this is impossible, but it is useful to speculate as to the outcome. When the three bifurcation factors are cross-tabulated with degrees of solidarity, there is a suggestion that all three contribute independently to the prediction.[2]

But would the subsistence types contribute independently to the result? Or would their contribution be exhausted by the bifurcation factors? Said another way, does the sheer distribution and character of the food supply have an independent effect on male solidarity, or does everything depend upon the manner in which the community organizes to exploit the environment? It was assumed at the outset that the natural systems do have a certain reactivity of their own that might be causal. Even if cross-tabulation showed no effect of subsistence type, it might still be argued that a developmental sequence is present, beginning with the natural systems and culminating in male solidarity. The question of whether this is indeed the direction of causation would still have to be faced, as is always so in correlational analysis. However, all these considerations are beside the point if another class of system—larger national organization—can be shown to influence the total structure of the community.

Subsistence Patterns and Levels of Articulation

Subsistence type has often been used alone as a measure of development from "savagery to civilization," as the English anthropologists

[2] That is, cases fall in the predicted cells, but there are too few to take seriously. Of course, even the other tables might not be statistically significant if such a criterion meant anything in a study of this sort and with this type of sample. Whatever validity may be claimed must depend upon the web of interpretations and illustrative tables, not on statistical arguments.

used to say. They reasoned that the increasing complexity of subsistence patterns, combined with the known sequence of their appearance in history, was sufficient grounds for their use as indices of evolution. But from the point of view of this study, subsistence base is only part of any developmental sequence; such a measure of development should indicate, among other things, the degree to which a community approximates the bifurcation pattern that is associated with variation in the subsistence pattern and that, it is hypothesized, leads directly to male solidarity. That is, the overall social organization must be tapped more directly.

Just such a measure may be available in what is probably the most important by-product of this study. Table 20 presents a scale of community complexity or, more precisely, what may be called village-national articulation. The details of its inception and construction have been published elsewhere (Young and Young 1962), and only the essentials need be given here. The initial conceptual basis of this measure was societal complexity, as proposed and operationalized by Freeman and Winch (1957). Their proposal derived in turn from Redfield's (1947) folk-urban typology.

However, preliminary results indicated that a more precise measure was possible, with fewer theoretical problems, if the community instead of the whole "society" is taken as the unit of analysis. Then the village or local band can be viewed as differentially participating in the larger national or colonial structure. This emphasis on articulation does not negate the previous interpretation in terms of complexity. On the contrary, the scale shows that institutional differentiation and the development of external contact are one and the same. If they were different, the various items could not be interlarded in the same scale. Moreover, each item in the scale can be interpreted as either internal or external development. Even a public square or dance area implies visitors, but the items concerning bureaucrats and religious specialists are even more convincing. In many cases these specialists come from outside the village and leave after several years. If, however, they are accepted by the villagers as part of the village structure, then their presence scales with little or no error. Said another way, the scaling technique demonstrates that all these apparently diverse items constitute a unidimensional measure, and inspection shows that they lead inevitably to greater articulation with the national structure.

TABLE **20.** Scale of **Community-Nation Articulation***

Step number	Item content	Percentage at each level
1	Two or more bisexual social or ceremonial gatherings of the local group per year.	100
2	Areas within the settlement pattern that are considered public—plaza, dance area, area around a public building, etc.	94
3	Structure that is used exclusively for non-domestic purposes—a temple or club-house, etc.	87
4	Crimes against persons or property punished by group action. Accused is formally charged, and there is a standard procedure of control. An effective colonial authority qualifies.	80
5	Symbolic medium of exchange—real money—in contrast to barter and exchange as the sole economic mechanism.	72
6	Fulltime bureaucrats unrelated to government head (in contrast to part-time bureaucrats related to government head, or lack of any).	65
7	Fulltime specialized real priest (not diviner or healer), including missionaries if they are at least partially accepted by community.	54
8	Written language used by at least one local person besides the priest	43
9	Formal education of both sexes with fulltime specialized teacher.	37
10	Local group has same culture as dominant society (in contrast to partially assimilated groups, ethnic subcultures, etc.).	11
Total cases		(54)

* Coefficient of scalability is .98

It is convenient, however, to trichotomize the scale into steps 1 to 3, reflecting the initial development of autonomy (although external communication is present even at this level); steps 4 to 8, reflecting a stage of contact in which the community is linked by particular roles; and the last two steps, 9 and 10, which are evidence of pervasive interpenetration with the urban world. These steps are associated with the mean estimated population of the communities, as shown in Table 21.

TABLE 21. **Population Characteristics of Three Articulation Levels**

Community-nation articulation level	Mean estimated community population		Judgment of modal tendency	
Local autonomy (steps 1-3)	133	(11)	Declining	(10)
Representative contact (steps 4-8)	307	(18)	Declining*	(16)
Urban interpenetration (steps 9-10)	867	(19)	Expanding	(19)
Total cases		(48)		(45)

* However, 5 were judged stationary, as compared to 7 declining and 4 expanding, indicating some stability. The modal tendency was unmistakable for the autonomous and interpenetrated communities.

Table 21 also shows the modal trend of population at these three levels. In general the largest communities are expanding and the smallest are declining. This association further supports the interpretation of the scale as one of articulation if we make the not unreasonable assumption that population expansion is facilitated by modern communications, business, and social organization, all of which tend more and more to be urban contributions.

The percentage of societies that fall into each level gives an important insight into the nature of this sample and of so-called primitive societies generally. The fact is that 37 per cent of this sample is quite civilized if formal education of both sexes is taken as a criterion. This level includes such groups as the Ooldea, Hopi, Yap, Nyakyusa, and Araucanians as well as the Lapps and Egyptians, the French and Americans. While it is true that ethnographers rarely mention the existence of a church or a school, the information can be found on maps or by close reading of prefaces. With rare exceptions the ethnographers wrote as if civilization never existed. It is not unfair to say that many of these reports are monuments to institutionalized selective inattention in field work.

If we follow the indication of the scale and assume that all the communities in the sample may be placed on a single dimension of community-national articulation, then a further shift of perspective is possible. We may hypothesize that the type of subsistence to a large extent determines the degree of articulation. From the point of view of the national or colonial organization, agricultural communities are worth more than food-gathering bands. They are more easily reached and controlled, and they may be organized into units of production. In return, the national government offers the benefits of civilization: trade, protection, education, and excitement. Whatever may be the destructive side of articulation, whether exploitation or disease, the fact remains that native peoples all over the world, regardless of the nationality of the invaders, have been deeply attracted to the ways of the newcomers. Thus, the local community typically strives for more, not less, articulation, and the more productive the community, the more likely it is to accomplish such articulation.

TABLE 22. **Relationship of Community-Nation Articulation Level to Subsistence Type**

	Modern agriculture	*Traditional agriculture*	*Horticulture*	*Food-gathering*
Local autonomy (steps 1-3)	0	11	21	56
Representative contact (steps 4-8)	0	56	53	33
Urban interpenetration (steps 9-10)	100	33	26	11
Total cases	(8)	(18)	(19)	(9)

Table 22 shows the levels of articulation reached by the societies in each of the four subsistence types. The interpretation above is supported by a strong linear association. The food-gatherers are typically articulated at the lowest levels, with the exception of the Ooldea of Australia, who have collected at a railroad junction and are almost totally dependent upon the government for food and welfare. On the other hand, the traditional agriculturalists and the horticulturalists are predominantly middle-level groups and as such corroborate the often repeated generalization that peasant communities may be characterized both in economic and in articulation terms. Among the traditional agriculturalists there are two deviant cases, the Nuer and the Siriono. The former are pasturalists whose nomadism inhibits articulation, while the Siriono, who grow some cereals but depend mainly on hunting and gathering, are barred from articulation by the exploitation and hostility of the whites in that area of Bolivia.

Articulation Level and Male Solidarity

How then does the articulation level of the community relate to institutionalized male solidarity? The hypothesis of a curvilinear relationship has been well stated by a number of previous writers. According to Murphy:

> This type society [in which men's cults occur] is simple and relatively undifferentiated. In such groups, the primary line of sex differentiation is not criss-crossed or blurred by multiple modes of role designation. Moreover, the division of labor is usually minimal—that is, between men and women. But we do not find the men's organization among the structurally most simple people in the world, such as the Polar Eskimo and Shoshone. It tends, rather, to occur in societies having larger local groups, in which economic coöperation is a stable and daily affair. In such a setting, members of each sex are in daily association and engage in common pursuits, frequently in coöperation, to the virtual exclusion of the other sex. In short, the sexes are true social groups, and the focus of social control over the women is vested in the males as a social entity [1959:96-97].

In this account Murphy is thinking of men's cults in basically the same manner in which they have been defined in this study; he is not referring to interest groups of the sort found in special sectors of complex societies. Therefore, his hypothesis lays special emphasis on the degree of role complexity that facilitates the formation of these stable community-wide groupings. In this form, hypotheses presented in this chapter relating subsistence types, collective male subsistence activity, warfare, etc., may now be seen as partial measures of middle-range role differentiation. Moreover, it has been shown empirically that the horticulturalists of the sort Murphy has in mind fall in the middle range of the articulation scale. The same relationship holds, although with greater variability, for the other indices of middle-range role complexity mentioned above.

It is important to note, however, that the articulation hypothesis carries the interpretation further. Community differentiation is not simply a by-product of a certain subsistence level that allows men more leisure time for interaction. Such an explanation does not, after all, explain why the men do not simply sit around and do nothing. Rather, the articulation interpretation accounts for the increasing role complexity and the bifurcation pattern of horticultural societies by emphasizing that national structures exert pressure toward the kind of social differentiation necessary for participation in a more complex structure and in modernization. In these terms the contribution of certain subsistence activities is to force various types of structural differentiation, which then may or may not be converted to the organizational coin of modernization. In general, the lack of role specialization in food-gathering groups is a handicap for the group and results these days in its extinction or dispersion, leaving individuals to participate, depending upon their capacities, in certain less organized sectors of the larger society. The horticultural societies have a better chance of participating, although the rigid institutionalization of some of them may work against it. Finally, small states or empires may have developed a division of labor such that an invading social system finds it feasible to take control of the whole structure. Perhaps the classic case of such total assimilation is the conquest of Mexico and Peru.[3]

It follows from the foregoing discussion that the articulation level should be a stronger predictor of male solidarity than any of those so far reviewed because it more adequately reflects the overall probability of bifurcation. Factors like warfare, subsistence activity, and the like lose their effect when not associated with other partial indicators. Thus, collective male subsistence activity makes less difference in horticultural societies, while multifemale family organization is quite important. But the articulation level supersedes these limited combinations and should give a clear result. Table 23 shows that it does indeed predict institutionalized male solidarity. The largest percentage of communities with male solidarity occurs in the middle levels of ar-

[3] Elman R. Service (1955) has reviewed the contact situation in South America and makes an analogous interpretation.

TABLE 23. **Degree of Male Solidarity by Community-Nation Articulation Level**

	Local autonomy (steps 1-3)	Representative contact (steps 4-8)	Urban interpenetration (steps 9-10)
Noninstitutionalized male solidarity (step 0)	82	48	60
Institutionalized male solidarity (steps 1-2)	0	17	15
Highly institutionalized male solidarity (steps 3-4)	18	35	25
Total cases	(11)	(23)	(20)

ticulation, where the link between village and nation is maintained by representatives such as the priest, the tax collector, the judge, and the merchant. Moreover, a large proportion of these cases show the highly institutionalized type of solidarity. It is too much to expect that all middle-level societies show solidarity of this form, for many other structures, such as the extended family or the traditional state, may alternate. It may be that the remaining 48 per cent have institutionalized structures which, while adapted to the stable conditions of the middle range, are incompatible with male cohesion.

But the occurence of male solidarity in autonomous and urbanized communities is contrary to the hypothesis. One of the two autonomous communities has already been encountered—the Nuer might have been more articulated but for their nomadism. The other group is the Kwakiutl of the Fort Rupert vicinity. From Boas' account no high level of articulation could be coded, but it is possible that he simply did not mention the presence of missionaries and similar representatives. By 1900 such links seem probable.

The communities with male solidarity that are highly articulated are, with the exception of the Egyptians, all at the ninth level. That is, they have formal education for both sexes, but they still speak a native dialect or are otherwise considered ethnic enclaves. These include the Balinese, Fijians, Hopi, Navaho, Ooldea, Tiv, and Yap. Moreover, four of them have highly institutionalized solidarity. Given this high proportion, it must be concluded that male solidarity can, under certain conditions, survive considerable contact with a national structure. But it is also possible that the form taken by articulation sometimes reinforces male solidarity as a defensive reaction to continued treatment as a second-rate ethnic group. Under such conditions, the men are in a situation not unlike that brought about by intercommunity warfare or collective hunting. If they are to avoid total disorganization, they have no recourse but to maintain a high degree of cooperation and solidarity. Perhaps, then, these deviant cases actually fit a generalized version of the hypothesis and are more the result of the insensitivity of the measure.

The effect of middle-level articulation may be rephrased as the consequence of a relationship between the local community and the nation that does not permit the smaller unit to participate fully in the urban structure. Whether it be the inadequate communication network of the city or active discrimination against an ethnic minority, the effect is the same because the local group is made to stand at a distance. The representatives pass from one unit to another, exchanging goods, collecting and loaning money, negotiating ideological compromises, and arranging an accommodation regarding the use of force, but the peasant community is left standing between the folk and urban worlds. On the other hand, just because it has the outside contact that it has, it can make fuller use of its resources. In many cases it achieves a long-term sedentary existence. In this context, intercommunity warfare may develop, bringing about another form of partial contact of which the most obvious effect is still further consolidation of the community. Male solidarity represents a further institutionalization of this enforced stability of societies of the middle range.

Summary

In interpreting any relationship like that found for dramatization and male solidarity, it is desirable to find the antecedent conditions of the presumed causal factor and to elucidate their sequence. Accordingly, male solidarity has been traced to those conditions of a community's social and natural environment that tend to favor the institutionalization of a male group which is separate from women and includes all the males of the community.

Although many particular factors within the community facilitate the development of solidarity, they all seem to operate within the general contexts of (1) the subsistence pattern, particularly horticulture and undeveloped traditional agriculture, and (2) the articulation level of the community. These two determinants are practically inseparable if it is true that, as argued here, contact with a larger social structure determines the degree to which local resources can be exploited.

In simplest terms, then, the relationship between the level of articulation, which is taken as the fundamental factor, and male solidarity is curvilinear. If a community has full participation in the urban structure, a complex division of labor develops that undermines the cumbersome community-wide male solidarity. On the other hand, until the middle levels of articulation are achieved, until the community has representative contact with other sociocultural systems, it may not achieve the stability required for the institutionalization of the sex groups. But such peasant stability is not to be viewed as a settled and secure plateau. Rather, it appears to be an uneasy truce between full participation in the urbanized world and the relative autonomy of the folk. When this marginal position is interpreted and then communicated to the villagers, male solidarity results: the men draw together for security, and they do not defect because there is no place to go.

6. The Dramatization of Female Sex Role and Parenthood

Since the publication of Van Gennep's book, it has been widely thought that the various rites of passage have much in common. To the extent that this is true, an explanation for one should hold for the others. And to the extent that a generalization holds in different empirical contexts, our confidence in it increases. For these reasons, to say nothing of our natural curiosity, it is of interest to apply the solidarity hypothesis to girls' initiations and to the social acceptance ceremonies associated with parenthood.

The Domestic Context of Female Solidarity

Chapter 1 has already shown that the ceremonies for girls fit the same scale that measures the elaboration of male ceremonies. To determine the empirical context of female solidarity is a more difficult problem. Following the lead given by male solidarity, the coders looked for village-wide organizations or activities that are exclusively female. These turned out to be rare. Organizational activity is present in only four communities, among the Cheyenne, Hopi, Samoans, and Yap. Similarly, only ten communities have women's work groups that include the majority of the adult women. But we already know that 31 communities have some degree of ceremonialization for girls. Clearly, these types of female solidarity, even if they are associated with the ceremonies, are not adequate predictors.

In anticipation of this paucity of community-wide female groupings, the schedule included questions about the presence of cooperative female groups based on proximity of households and domestic work. Only exclusively female work groups were coded. Although the degree of supervision and the frequency of cooperation were studied, these did not discriminate except to exclude from the classification the occasional neighboring of women in modernized communities.

In practice, cooperation is confined to the functioning domestic unit —whether the nuclear family or a homestead with an extended family —and the kind of work varies from cooking to gardening. In all, 25 communities have exclusive female work groups organized around domestic tasks and involving regular cooperation. The presence of such groups is related to female dramatization, but the association is not strong, and adding the few cases of village-wide female cooperative activity does not greatly improve it. Indeed, a stronger relationship holds between degrees of female dramatization and multifemale household organization, even though at this point there is no good reason for interpreting such household organization as female solidarity.

The weak correlation of female domestic work groups and dramatization is not unexpected. It will be recalled that male work groups are not strong predictors of boys' initiation ceremonies. The crucial factor in the case of males is the institutionalization of male activity to the point where they have a sense of unity and definite social boundaries. It is therefore reasonable to ask what the equivalent factor for women is. Could it be that under certain conditions the domestic establishment itself becomes the unit of organization?

Certainly in many communities the women are left to themselves in compounds or isolated camps day after day. If these households are in fact socially separated from other similar units, the women might readily come to see themselves as a solidary unit maintaining a definition of their situation in opposition to that held by other groups of women. One indicator of such a crystallized group image would be a wall or similar barrier around the domestic establishment. Another indicator would be a central symbolic focus such as a shrine, a house crest, or other physical representation of household unity. Because information on boundaries is so often missing, as the result perhaps of the maintenance of social distance without a physical barrier, the indicators of household focus were considered alternates. Thus, 23 communities were coded as "bounded" or "focused" in that they had some physical barrier around the domestic site or in that a definite local symbol of membership was present.

As expected, institutionalized household solidarity, as we may now call it, is a strong predictor of girls' initiation ceremonies. But the clearest picture is given by combining such solidary households with the presence of overt cooperation among the women so that a typology of what will be labeled female solidarity is formed. Thus the empirical context of female solidarity is the regular cooperation of women in an institutionalized household. It is typically an infracommunity grouping, although quite often the compound or homestead may be equivalent to a community.

Table 24 throws additional light on the nature of female solidarity by showing its marked association with multifemale family organization. The latter index combines the extent of polygyny with the prevalence of extended families. As has been noted, there is considerable overlap between extended families and polygynous families, and Table 24 simply extends our knowledge of these large families by showing that there is also active work organization and the symbolization of household unity. And inasmuch as the women in these compounds typically have their own huts, separate from their husbands, it is apparent that there is a definite separation of the sexes and a strict division of labor. What seems to emerge is a picture of the corporate family. Murdock has already asserted this overall structural pattern in his coding of extended families (1957:668), and the present typology refines this grouping by cutting out some extended families that are not institutionalized and by adding some polygynous families that are. Needless to say, many of these corporate families are localized kin groups and are therefore equivalent to what Murdock has called clan communities.

The close association of the typology of female solidarity with customs that bring many women into one household explains why the latter pattern predicted girls' initiation ceremonies. The presence of many women indirectly taps female solidarity. But Table 24 shows a *decrease* in the association in the fourth type, precisely where one would expect it to be greatest. If this were an isolated instance, it might be attributed to normal variation since the cases are so few; but, as subsequent sections will show, the curvilinear pattern is quite persistent.

TABLE 24. **Relationship of Multifemale Household Organization to Type of Female Solidarity**

	I *Neither female work groups nor institution-alized household unity*	II *Female work groups only*	III *Institution-alized house-hold unity only*	IV *Female work groups and institution-alized house-hold unity*
Multifemale household organization	24	33	90	77
Total cases	(17)	(12)	(10)	(13)

Analogizing from the results of male solidarity, it may be hypothesized that corporate families, and the female solidarity that is usually associated with them, are more solidary in the middle levels of articulation and less so in the upper levels. What happens is that as the larger community articulates with the wider society, its control and protection are extended to the constituent domestic units. Homesteads begin to hire male labor and to diversify their production, and customs involving multiple women, either polygyny or large extended families, tend to change. More fundamentally, the integration of the domestic unit into the community makes it increasingly impossible to maintain the highly institutionalized definition of the unit that once was functional. However, when this hypothesis is actually tested, the result is negative. That is, when articulation is trichotomized as before and used to predict the occurrence of the four types of female solidarity, there is no definite difference in the proportions.

On the face of it, the hypothesis should be abandoned, but three considerations justify more patience. In the first place there is a trend when the indicator of institutionalization—a bounded or focused household—is taken alone, suggesting that the typology as a whole may be a weak indicator of general structure. Second, the precision of the typology is blunted by the fact that it must be based on the typical family pattern. In articulated communities family structure may be quite variable. Third and more pressing is the fact that solidarity within the family unit is quite different from village-wide male olidarity. If articulation is a measure of the integration of the community into the larger national structure, it may be that a subsystem ike the family does not feel the effects of this change so rapidly or decisively. Or, looking at the lowest level of articulation, in comparison to male solidarity the solidary family may more readily survive under these conditions of mobility. It will be useful to reassess this question after more evidence on family structure has been presented.

Girls' Initiation Ceremonies

With the shift of the unit of solidarity taken into account, the explanation of female initiation dramatization is the same as that for males. Girls grow up in the domestic establishment and are adequately socialized for work and marriage by the time they reach early adolescence. But in communities where corporate families are typical, the girls must also learn to take part in the tightly organized group of women that dominates everyday affairs. Regardless of any rule of residence that may take her to another such group, a girl must learn to submit to the authority of the elder women, to do her part of the work, and ultimately to contribute to the ongoing unit while maintaining a certain autonomy in her own hut and among her own children.

To facilitate this role-learning, the women of the household arrange a dramatization of the transition from girlhood to preadulthood, and the more institutionalized the family, the more elaborate the ceremony. However, because the unit of solidarity is smaller, the ceremonies are rarely as elaborate as those for boys. Similarly, they are less likely to involve the whole community or to focus on a group of initiates. As with boys, the function of the initiation ceremony is to allow the girl access to the female backstage, to all the whispers and innuendos and sharp lines of authority that make this side of family life so different from the protected child's world. Moreover, the ceremony alerts the women to the change in status so that they change their attitude toward the girl and, so to speak, stop lowering their voices when she is near.

This hypothesis is tested in Table 25. The dramatization scale is trichotomized as was done for males, and all four types of female solidarity are shown. The association generally supports the hypothesis, but type IV solidarity fails to differentiate between the highest degrees of dramatization.

TABLE 25. **Relationship of Degree of Female Sex-Role Dramatization to Type of Female Solidarity**

	I	II	III	IV
	Neither female work groups nor institutionalized household unity	*Female work groups only*	*Institutionalized household unity only*	*Female work groups and institutionalized household unity*
Undramatic sex-role recognition (step 0)	59	58	40	8
Individualized dramatization (steps 1-2)	41	25	30	46
Group dramatization (steps 3-4)	0	17	30	46
Total cases	(17)	(12)	(10)	(13)

As a check on the tentatively proposed explanation of this blunting of the predictive power of female solidarity, we may cross-tabulate levels of articulation with degrees of dramatization. The assumption is that the latter measure is a more accurate and sensitive indicator and should reflect the weakening of corporate family structure even though the corporate "shell," as indicated by walls and shrines, may persist. This hypothesis is tested in Table 26, which does show the familiar curvilinear effect of articulation on the most elaborate female initiation ceremonies.

A further check on this interpretation is provided by the seven cases of type IV solidarity that do not have group dramatization of the girls' status. Five of these seven communities are articulated at the lowest or the highest but not at the middle level. In contrast, half of the six cases that have the most elaborate dramatization are from the

TABLE 26. **Relationship of Degree of Female Sex-Role Dramatization to Community-Nation Articulation Level**

	Local autonomy (steps 1-3)	*Representative contact (steps 4-8)*	*Urban interpenetration (steps 9-10)*
Undramatic role sex-recognition (step 0)	46	39	45
Individualized dramatization (steps 1-2)	36	35	40
Group dramatization (steps 3-4)	18	26	15
Total cases	(11)	(23)	(20)

middle levels. Thus, the deviant cases are partially explained by the adverse social organization of the community in which the corporate family operates. When a more sensitive measure of female solidarity is devised, it should reduce the variability of this relationship.

The Dramatization of Parenthood

There is yet another ceremony widespread in traditional communities that may be explained by the solidarity hypothesis. Called the "couvade" by some investigators, the cluster of customs that surround the birth of children, especially the first child, has been the object of much puzzlement and not a little nonsense. The term *couvade* was assigned to what early writers took to be the husband's imitation of his wife's behavior during pregnancy. Thus, if a husband restricted his activities, he was said to be imitating his wife's debility. In the extremely stereotyped interpretations, the husband was even thought to experience morning sickness.

Norbeck (1961:142ff.) has succinctly reviewed the variations in the interpretations of these customs, and two points emerge quite clearly. The first is that while writers talk of the restrictions on husbands and on wives and interpret these variously as symbolic representations of social paternity, community expectations, or individual anxiety, the cluster of customs preceding and following the birth of a child is nonetheless called a *birth* crisis and is typically discussed as the first ceremony in the life cycle. There is a contradiction in such treatment because logically the customs should focus on the child if it is his life cycle that is being discussed. It is probable that in all societies infants are treated as nonpersons; the real object of the ceremony is the parents, and the form the ritual takes is basically similar to that taken by the initiation ceremonies already considered.

The second point that emerges is that, like so many hypotheses in this field, the available interpretations concentrate on the *meaning* of the ceremony. While social meaning is inextricably embedded in the function of a custom, it seems an unwise strategy to focus on this subtle aspect and to push the problem of determining the objective conditions of its occurrence into the background.

In the present study the technique of Guttman scaling was applied to this problem, with the result shown in Table 27. Although still a short scale by strict standards, it compensates for this weakness by a coefficient of scalability of .88. As before, the items disregard all but the general content, and the attributes must be group-wide. The latter requirement eliminates such modern customs as sprinkling or the presentation of the child at the temple.

Step 0 is a residual category and was not specifically coded. It includes all the minor and transient customs like food fads of pregnant women and standard remarks about the likeness of the child to his father. Step 1, ritual concern for the newborn, is quite widespread. In this scale it must be interpreted as the counterpart to the minimum social recognition given parents. It is probably impossible to code such role recognition directly because it is not consistently reported. Steps 2 and 3 form a pair specifying the ritual behavior of the parents during the pregnancy period. Although restriction of the mother is more frequent, the scale shows that both parents must behave as dictated by community custom. The items therefore reflect a reciprocal interaction of the married couple and the community. Steps 4 and 5 also form a pair because they specify the ritual behavior of both parents in a second crucial time period. However, step 5 is more specific than 4 because it was impossible to distinguish the mother's ritual behavior from the normal disability of the post-partum period. Had this been possible, another step could have been inserted between 3 and 4.

One other item, mentioned by Radcliffe-Brown (1956:146-47) and

TABLE **27. Scale of Dramatization of Parenthood**

Step number	Item content	Percentage of sample communities
0	No community-wide ritual requirements or prohibitions on parents before or after birth or directed toward newborn, or informal ones only	100
1	Special attention or concern for welfare of newborn other than normal cleansing	88
2	Ritual restrictions or requirements on mother during pregnancy period	73
3	Ritual restrictions or requirements on father during pregnancy period	56
4	Ritual restrictions or requirements on father after birth of child	33
5	Seclusion of mother at time of birth or immediately thereafter	14
Total cases*		(52)

* Data are lacking for the Mixtec and Lapps.

discussed by Tylor (1961:4ff.), might have scaled had it been included in the data collection schedule. That is the practice of teknonymy. As Tylor describes it:

> Among these [Cree] Indians the young husband, coming to live with his wife's parents, must turn his back on them, not speaking to them (especially not to his mother-in-law), being thus treated as a stranger till his first child is born; whereupon he takes its name, and is called "father of So-and-so," and thenceforth attaches himself to his parents-in-law rather than to his own parents. That is to say, he is ceremonially treated as a stranger till his child, being born a member of the family, gives him a status as father of a member of the family, whereupon they consistently leave off the farce of not recognizing him [1961:5].

Tylor gives evidence of an association between teknonomy and matrilocal residence, but the present study would emphasize the association of this and the other customs of parenthood dramatization with the highly solidary family. The hypothesis is the same as that already tested for male and female initiation ceremonies except that the unit of analysis changes. For female solidarity the corporate group is only the context within which female solidarity develops and is itself of no direct concern, but the explanation of a ceremony for a married pair must take the family structure as its point of reference. In such a tightly coordinated domestic organization a newly married couple is not fully accepted until the first child is born. The entrance ceremony is linked to this event because children are important for the work and continuance of the family, and a marriage that is unfruitful is not likely to survive the pressure for children. Moreover, many other adjustments make a new marriage unstable during the first few years; and if the marriage is dissolved, the complicated ties between two large families, often involving considerable exchange of wealth, must also be severed.

Consequently, it does not pay to take the young couple fully into the group until a child is born, but when this event occurs, it must be publicly helped over the threshold by the dramatization of its new status. This hypothesis holds even for American society, although in a less elaborate way. The baby showers and ritual smoking of cigars signal membership in a new network of communications. Rather suddenly the couple is invited to homes that had previously been closed, and the flow of advice and baby gadgets confirms the links. This increased social interaction is punctuated by exaggerated use of the status terms "mother" and "father," all liberally coated with saccharine sentiment.

The test of the application of the solidarity hypothesis to the dramatization of parenthood might have used the typology of female solidarity as an indicator of institutionalized family structure, and in fact an adequate relationship does exist—although the familiar curvilinear pattern is present. But this typology was constructed for a somewhat different purpose, and a more direct indicator is at hand. Murdock's coding of clan organization[1] not only includes the typical corporate family of interest here, but takes into consideration several other crucial indicators of corporate groups: their localization and control of land, their organization as a productive unit, and their tendency to-

[1] Ethnographic atlas, 1962. Data for the present sample are contained in column 64 of the code.

ward exogamy and unilineal descent. Moreover, Murdock's code recognizes the segmentation that typically occurs when population size increases, and he classifies such groups separately. Thus a control on articulation is nicely built into the code, enabling us to see the inhibiting effect of the wider community organization. Table 28 exhibits the relationship.

TABLE 28. **Relationship of Parenthood Dramatization to Clan Organization**

	No clan organization	Segmented clan organization	Exogamous or clan communities
Undramatic or minimal recognition of parenthood (steps 0-1)	40	17	23
Dramatization during pregnancy (steps 2-3)	30	56	31
Post-partum dramatization (steps 4-5)	30	28	46
Total cases	(20)	(18)	(13)

In the clan communities and those with a rule of exogamy there is the increase in the percentage of the more elaborate parenthood ceremonies that the hypothesis leads one to expect. The relationship indirectly confirms the interpretation of the relatively isolated (i.e., unsegmented) groups as the most corporate, and, in fact, five of the seven cases with post-partum dramatization of parenthood (step 5) fall in this middle level of articulation.

Alternative Interpretations of Parenthood Ceremonies

How does this explanation compare to that of others? Three representative positions are those of Van Gennep, Radcliffe-Brown, and Whiting. Van Gennep (1960:41ff.) proposed that pregnancy and birth customs exemplify his three phases of transition. In general the evidence of the scale does not support his contention. Of course, the scale may not cover all the customs that Van Gennep might have included, nor does it interpret particular customs in terms of his phases. On the other hand, it is difficult to see how a ceremony at the level of step 1 or step 2 could include rites of separation, transition, and integration. It would not be elaborate enough.

Radcliffe-Brown, in a second conceptualization (1956:150-51), is more interested in the meaning of the pregnancy rituals, which for him tends to converge on the aspects of the environment that are important in the life of the people. Thus, food taboos call attention to a person's ritual status and also remind him of the value of these foods. The scale does not contradict such an interpretation, but its emphasis on formal patterns leaves it with little to say about the values reflected in the particular observances. This scale, like its counterpart for initiation, supports the notion of ritual status but does not go beyond this to the more specific meanings that may be present.

A third conception of pregnancy and birth rituals is that they reflect the imitation of the wife by her husband. In view of the kinds of items included in the scale, this interpretation seems forced, but it is always possible that the relevant items were omitted from the original data pool. As a check on this possibility the coders made a special search for any custom that appeared to reflect imitative behavior. They found only two relevant cases. Among the Timbira the husband must walk around the house during the birth of his child, and in general his movements are restricted. The Camayura require the father to stay in his house for a month after the birth of the baby. In the other 50 communities for which data exist, the husband did nothing that could be considered "lying in."

Given this lack of evidence, the question is raised as to why any of these customs should have been interpreted as imitation. Even if one disregards past misinterpretations of deficient ethnographic data, current belief in the theory is reinforced by the occurrence of the phenomenon among psychiatric patients. In this particular variation of hysteria the patient complains of morning sickness, aches and pains, and so forth, and may connect his troubles to those of a pregnant wife.[2] The argument becomes, then, that the occurrence of this custom in primitive societies is simply a normalization of what in modern society occurs only as a symptom complex. But is this a valid

2 Although no citation is at hand, accounts of this symptom pattern are not rare in clinical circles.

ssumption? Even in a community where the father observes ritual estrictions during his wife's pregnancy, would his claims of pain and morning sickness be accepted as real? It would be useful to have reliable ethnographic evidence on this point; it seems likely that the behavior is taken as symbolic and that the other men would regard a father who actually believed he was "sick" in the same way in which he would be regarded in industrial societies, that is, as obviously deviant.

A more accurate analogy to primitive parenthood rituals is the modern custom of "rooming in," in which a mother is secluded with her child in a private room, where she can be visited freely by her husband. This elaboration of family custom is mainly a middle-class development, but the excitement and attention involved are perhaps not different in kind from that to be found in the more sociable post-partum settings of rural or lower-class large families. Neither of these modern patterns is comparable, however, to the symptom complex of hysterical husbands.

Whiting and his associates (Burton and Whiting 1961, Munroe 1959) have proposed an explanation for the imitation concept of birth customs in keeping with their theory of initiation ceremonies. They posit, it will be recalled, that an exclusive mother-son sleeping arrangement gives rise to a feminine identification in the boy. This, in combination with patrilocal residence, results in a conflict as to role that is finally resolved by the initiation ceremony in favor of male identification. In combination with matrilocal residence, on the other hand, the initial feminine identification is reinforced rather than resolved, and it expresses itself later in a man's life by behavior imitative of his pregnant or nursing wife.

A moment's thought convinces one that, even if true, the hypothesis is inadequate for handling the kind of parenthood ceremony indexed by the scale in Table 27, for the occurrence of the particular combination of determinants designated by Whiting is quite limited. If one decodes exclusive mother-son sleeping arrangements by following Whiting's conceptual scheme but omitting vague data, and uses Murdock's classification of matrilocal (including avunculocal) residence, only four out of 43 societies have both. All four of these communities do indeed have parenthood ceremonies, but 28 societies that also have the ceremonies are left unexplained. It seems probable that the combination of matrilocal residence and exclusive mother-son sleeping arrangements (typical of the separate mother-son households of corporate families) is simply an indirect measure of family institutionalization, but the restricted range of Whiting's explanation makes comparison impossible except with a much larger sample.

A Related Custom: Post-Partum Taboo and the Corporate Family

The custom of the post-partum taboo could be interpreted as a parenthood restriction, but it does not form part of the "birth crisis" and so was not discussed above. This custom—whereby the nursing mother is prohibited from sexual intercourse for as long as two or three years —though strange to Western ears, occurs in about half the communities of the sample. The native interpretations of the practice are various: that sexual intercourse sours the mother's milk, that it harms the child, that it is generally dangerous, and so on. This sort of mythological overlay of a custom is, of course, typical in all societies and far from facilitating understanding, simply adds further social facts that require explanation.

On the face of it, the practice operates to space children.[3] In societies in which a mother must work hard, it is a burden to have children too frequently. But if that were the sole explanation, we should expect the custom to be more widespread than it is. It is true that infanticide may be a functional equivalent in some societies, but that possibility simply deepens the problem of explaining why certain societies practice the post-partum taboo rather than an equivalent custom. The hypothesis that is suggested by the earlier discussion of corporate families is that such child-spacing is especially important in situations where the mother must work regularly in tasks that are important to a larger group. This is the case in many homesteads and compounds in which each woman has her own hut and garden and must feed her own children as well as contribute to the group larder. Under these conditions, even if she did have milk for several children they would be a hindrance to her gardening.

We should not suppose, however, that the custom is the recurrent

[3] It is so considered in, for example, Davis and Blake (1956).

outcome of rational analysis on the part of the hard-working mother. On the contrary, the decision is made for her by the structural arrangements of most corporate groups. Where there is polygyny and the separation of the sleeping quarters of the sexes, the husband cannot be in constant association with his wife anyway. When an infant arrives, the separation already built into the system is simply accentuated. We should thus expect to find the post-partum taboo less often in nomadic groups. Their mobility probably operates similarly to the way in which the work pressure of sedentary groups operates; but infanticide is more adaptable to the extreme conditions of nomadism, and in the nomadic families there is no organizational reinforcement of this taboo. However, it might very well occur on an individual basis.

This explanation for the post-partum taboo is tested in Table 29, which relates clan organization to the presence of the custom. As before, we expect a lesser proportion of the segmented communities to have this taboo because clan organization tends to weaken in large, articulated places.

TABLE 29. **Relationship of Post-Partum Taboo to Clan Organization**

	No clan organization	Segmented clan organization	Exogamous or clan communities
Presence of post-partum taboo of any duration	30	58	83
Total cases	(20)	(19)	(12)

Post-partum taboo shows, if anything, a curvilinear association with parenthood dramatization and female initiation. Inasmuch as the latter two attributes are linearly related—as we should expect, given their similar status as indicators and their freedom from the influence of articulation—the complete explanation of the post-partum taboo is not yet at hand. Either more refined coding of the custom or the discovery of special conditions under which it is practiced seems necessary.

Nonetheless, a possible strategy for the analysis of corporate groups is opened up. If other similar items could be found, they may combine into an accurate measure of corporateness. Some possible candidates are the sororate, the levirate, certain types of ancestor worship, bride price, inheritance rules, and various taboos that separate the sexes. Unilinear descent might also be a usable attribute if it is analyzed into its components, as Fried (1957) has done, and if recognition is given to the variety of other ways of symbolizing group membership. If the solidarity hypothesis does in fact apply to families, the various customs should increasingly reflect the crystallization of the group's definition of its situation.

Summary

This chapter examines the solidarity hypothesis as it applies to girls' initiations and to parenthood ceremonies. The test is complicated by the fact that women do not typically organize at the village level, so female solidarity must be studied where it does occur, within the context of the domestic unit. To measure female solidarity a typology was constructed by combining the presence of exclusively female domestic work groups with the presence of some physical elaboration of family boundaries or unity. The four combinations given by these two factors are in fact associated with degrees of female sex-role dramatization as measured by the scale presented in Chapter 1. The higher steps in the female solidarity typology reflect a state of household institutionalization that may be considered corporate. These families show the traditional earmarks of corporateness in that they are localized production units that have developed symbols of unity such as unilinear descent or a norm of exogamy. Additionally, they typically have a strict division of labor between the sexes and customs like polygyny or extended family organization that involve a large number of female workers.

The clan concept, which overlaps with the delineation of highly institutionalized families, was used as an alternative indicator. It is particularly applicable to the prediction of parenthood dramatization in that it more adequately taps the overall family unit, which is the specific system of reference for this custom. In order to maintain the solidarity of the corporate family, an entrance ceremony is necessary for new nuclear units. This ceremony usually occurs at the birth of the first child, and its elaboration may be measured by a scale analogous to those applied to male and female initiation ceremonies. The association of corporate families with parenthood dramatization shows that the solidarity hypothesis may be generalized to other situations.

Another custom, the post-partum taboo on a mother's sex relations, is also associated with corporate family organization, and the relationship adds to our understanding of the ways in which such dramatic ways of delineating social meanings are required by solidary groups.

7. Family, Community, and Social Change

The conceptual forecast given in Chapter 5 suggested that some societies would be found that are sexually bifurcated in the sense that each sex forms a group organized on a community-wide basis. It was not expected that the women would have clubhouses and the like, but the data were collected in the hope that the solidarity of females within family and work groups could be shown to extend in a kind of informal network across the community. It is now clear that female solidarity is not in the usual case so extended. Rather, the cohesion of females appears to be an aspect of the highly institutionalized family, and such family structures seem to develop under conditions of relative isolation.

The findings thus require a revision of the notion of bifurcation as it was previously conceived. Although the term may be retained, it must now be thought of as a relationship between two levels of organization—family and local community—rather than as an interaction of two subgroups of equal status. These relationships naturally call for analysis, but they also raise a prior question: could it be that male solidarity is simply an aspect of solidary communities, analogous to the relationship between female solidarity and the highly institutionalized family, and that the relationship between male and female solidarity should be reconceptualized as one between family and community?

A Typology of Family and Community Relationships

It is a reasonable view, and the ethnographic literature supports it, that communities with male solidarity are quite cohesive. It will be recalled that the scale of solidarity included the presence of a boundary-maintaining activity, a religious aspect to this activity, ranking of the participants, and training for war. By definition the scale included only village-wide activities. The possibility that the men maintain other religious activity, other kinds of ranking, etc., was allowed, but in fact such organization is rare. The exceptions are of the sort found in some African societies, where some of the community-wide religious activity includes women or where royalty requires a deference system apart from that ordinarily practiced by the men. The general situation of communities with strong male solidarity is that other community-wide networks of social relationships are absent or weak; all community activity finds its focus in that of the men. Where community-wide lineage, female, or authority relationships are competitive, the community was usually found to be involved in a major structural transition.

The reformulation suggests a typology of communities constructed in terms of the presence or absence of cohesive families and of male solidarity, the latter factor now taken as equivalent to over-all community solidarity. Table 30 shows the four combinations. It was constructed by dichotomizing the typology of family types into two categories, those with a symbolic focus or a norm of separation (highly institutionalized) as opposed to those without these indicators. The actual work cooperation of females, which also forms part of the criteria for the typology, was ignored for present purposes. Correspondingly, the scale of male solidarity was divided into the general categories of uninstitutionalized solidarity versus any degree of solidarity represented by the four scale steps.

Type I, where there are neither solidary families nor a solidary community, includes most of the modernized places and some of the very small, nomadic groups.

Type II is the pure case of the cohesive community where males are organized and dominant and the family is subordinate. One thinks of the small hamlet communities of New Guinea and many other parts of the world, where mutual raiding or certain types of subsistence activity require a high degree of community discipline and where the unit is small enough to allow such total social control. In fact, five of the nine cases are located in the Pacific area. The four that are not—Cheyenne, Hopi, Ooldea, Timbira—seem to show much the same over-all community cohesiveness.

TABLE 30.   **Typology of Communities Based on the Relationship Between Community (Male) and Family (Female) Solidarity**

FEMALE SOLIDARITY	MALE SOLIDARITY	
	Absent (step 0)	Present (steps 1-4)
Absent (types I and II)	I (20)	II (9)
Present (types III and IV)	III (11)	IV (12)
Total cases	(31)	(21)

Type III, although also a specialized type, may in practice take many forms. Highly institutionalized families appear under nomadic conditions if these conditions allow some degree of group unity and identification; the Chiricahua Apache and Jivaro fall in this category. Otherwise, most of these cases may be characterized as showing the homestead pattern—that is, they are scattered compounds that enjoy the protection of a wider pattern of social control. Significantly, six of the 11 cases are African.

Type IV, where both solidary community and family are present, is represented by 12 cases. These are the Balinese, Camayura, Chagga, Dahomeans, Egyptians, Kwakiutl, Navaho, New Irelanders (Lesu), Nuer, Samoans, Thonga, and Tiv. There is no concentration in any one continent, nor is their articulation level decisively different from that of types II and III. From what has already been said of the conditions under which the two kinds of solidarity occur, one may presume that these bifurcated communities of type IV allow enough separation between families for family institutionalization to develop, but not so much that male solidarity is curtailed.

One may readily imagine more elaborate typologies of community structure. The ramifications of lineage affiliation may be such that both the over-all and the family organization of the community are obscured, and what at first was an interstitial structure comes to be the backbone of the unit. Such an interpretation is in accord with the lack of association between the three categories of clan organization discussed in the previous chapter and either male or female solidarity.

Similarly, interest groups may multiply, as in Dahomey, to the extent that one is inclined to see the whole community as a lattice of sub-groups that are neither family nor community-wide, though a much larger sample and more detailed coding would be required for analysis of secondary structures of this sort. It remains true, however, that the typology given above represents the basic structural axis for cross-cultural study and is the first step in any analysis of the kinds of structural change that may take place.

Bifurcated Societies and Structural Change

The bifurcation typology poses in a new form the question of antecedent conditions. Previous chapters inquired about one or the other form of solidarity; now we ask about the conditions under which the combinations may occur. A new element is introduced because it is possible that the interaction of the highly institutionalized family and the community is a significant factor in any course of change that may occur. Certainly the hypothesis of antagonism between the solidary family and the wider structures that impinge upon it has long been accepted in sociological circles.[1] The structure of the American family, which is considered to be the extreme case of capitulation to and penetration by any and all organizations in the wider community, is typically interpreted as having failed to maintain its earlier autonomy; and the basic hypothesis may easily be extended to the case of a large family group that comes under the control of a solidary community.

The over-all picture that is suggested is a progressive capitulation of the autonomy of the smaller unit to that of a larger superseding structure, although a certain delimited area of "states' rights" typically remains. In the extreme case, one might expect a cyclical process whereby a given unit tends toward a high degree of solidarity and autonomy, but then loses to a larger unit of social control, and so on. Speculation about such an ideal sequence suggests the further hypothesis that the very drive toward autonomy so characteristic of solidary groups forces it into interaction with others, thereby hastening its integration into the wider structure. One immediately thinks of

[1] See the discussion of this hypothesis in Greenfield (1961).

lineage affiliations, which at first are symbolic of group unity but may ramify to link many segments and thereby become the foundation for a wider unit of social control.

By and large the data of this study are inadequate for the analysis of such a process. Cross-cultural studies, like other comparative designs, are "flat," and time depth is obtained only by roundabout inferences. Nonetheless, it is in order to consider what information is available, if only to expose the methodological problem that is posed.

Beginning with the hypothesis that antagonism develops between solidary groups operating in the same social context at adjacent system levels, one notes that the presence of 12 examples of type IV argues against an extreme version of the hypothesis. If the highly institutionalized family and the solidary community cannot occur together because of inherent conflict, we should not have found these cases. Moreover, different cutting points did not eliminate them. Neither did the cross-tabulation of degrees of male and female dramatization, which are more sensitive indices of solidarity, reveal a different association.

It may still be argued that the effect of this antagonism is slight, requiring a more sensitive measure. It is possible to test this if we compare the percentage of elaborate male and female initiation ceremonies in the four community types. The assumption is that the ceremonies reflect the strength of the solidary structures; hence, any weakening of them should bring about a reduction of the ceremonies. Of course it would not do to look at initiation ceremonies of any degree of elaboration; the definition of the typology would then determine the result. But taking the highest steps in the scale (3 and 4) ought to reveal differences. In particular, one would expect the percentage of such elaborate ceremonies to be lower in type IV, where the conflict presumably is greatest, than in types II and III. Table 31, which exhibits these facts, shows, on the contrary, that the percentage in type IV is not less. The inference therefore is that, relative to types II and III, the solidary structures of type IV communities are going concerns and are not weakened by their juxtaposition in the same social context.

By these two tests the hypothesis that the autonomous family and the community are mutually incompatible structures is rejected, but it may still be that they exist together only under special conditions.

TABLE 31. **Percentage of Elaborate Dramatization Ceremonies in Four Community Types**

	Community type	Number of cases*	Elaborate male drama- tization (steps 3-4)	Elaborate female dra- matization (steps 3-4)
I	Nonsolidary family and community	(20)	0	10
II	Solidary community only	(9)	44	0
III	Solidary family only	(11)	9	36
IV	Both family and community solidarity	(12)	42	42
Total cases		(52)		

* These figures are the base for each of the percentages at the right. Thus, none of the 20 type I communities has elaborate male dramatization, and only 10 per cent have elaborate ceremonials for girls.

Although no evidence is available on the point, the type IV communities may all show a common settlement pattern—one of intercommunicating small locality groups, in contrast to a compact village pattern, nomadic bands, or dispersed homesteads under the control of a wider community organization. It may be that such a settlement pattern facilitates the double arrangement. This interpretation is reinforced by at least one fact: a higher proportion (50 per cent) of type IV communities engage in either modern or transitional agriculture than do type II (22 per cent) or type III (36 per cent) communities. Needless to say, type I communities have the highest proportion (65 per cent).

What of the second hypothesis that is implicit in the picture of solidary structures given above? Regardless of any interaction between family and community, it may still be that the whole community is at the mercy of wider systems of social control. Increased articulation in a national social structure should bring about the termination of any small autonomous structure. There is, in fact, a tendency for the three types that include solidary structures to be included in the middle ranges of the articulation scale, in contrast to type I, which on the whole is articulated at either the highest or the lowest levels. This same contrast between type I and the others holds also for multifemale family organization and type of warfare. Type I communities rarely have elaborate forms of multifemale organization, while the other three types typically do; similarly, type I communities are less likely to be engaged in local warfare. With respect to rule of residence, type I communities are like those with solidary families only (type III) in that about 20 per cent of them have an ambilocal pattern, in contrast to the more strongly unilocal rules of types II and IV.

Only the mean estimated population seems to differentiate among the types. Showing much the same pattern as the subsistence categories mentioned above, type IV communities have an average population size of 677, in contrast to 597, 343, and 117 for types I, II, and III respectively. The only other factor that might discriminate among the types is settlement pattern, as discussed and qualified above. These characteristics suggest that type IV communities are in a certain sense transitional. In contrast to the "pure" types represented by II and III, type IV communities are larger and more integrated into the cereal-growing subsistence pattern characteristic of modernizing areas. If the articulation scale were more sensitive and the sample larger, we might find these communities falling in the upper levels (steps 7 and 8) of the middle range.

The Decline of Initiation Ceremonies

The direct evidence of the decline of initiation ceremonies given in the ethnographies opens another line of attack on both the problem of whether civilization makes solidary families and communities impossible and the prior question of whether dramatization is actually related to solidarity. If the initiation ceremony of a given society has declined, male solidarity should also have declined. Furthermore, the level of articulation should have moved to some higher step. Although a direct analysis of change over time would provide the strongest support for these hypotheses, the possibilities of such a test are extremely limited in cross-cultural research. Only the fact that initiation ceremonies are striking events, easily remembered by native informants and often inquired about by ethnographers, makes even a rudimentary test possible.

Decline of initiation ceremonies involves a change in or disappearance of customs such that a different scale step appears. In practice the change is from some degree of dramatization to none. This variable was coded directly from the ethnographic reports on the basis of a statement by either the ethnographer or an informant that the ceremony had declined in recent years—usually in the last generation—or, more directly, on the basis of evidence of a change in the customs. If the customs had entirely disappeared, the coder's inference was simple. More problematic were the instances of a perfunctory ceremony (circumcision) at the age of six or seven. Fortunately, most of these cases were accompanied by a statement that it was once held at a later age and was surrounded by a well-defined ritual.

It proved impossible to code decline of male solidarity. Although there are some adequate reports on former men's houses, etc., the general lack of information one way or the other undermined reliable coding. An attempt was made to code decline of local warfare, on which information is fairly even. The results have already been presented in Table 11, but when they were cross-tabulated with decline of initiation, the cases that were clearly interpretable were too few—although the result was in the right direction. If the coding of supracommunity warfare were refined to distinguish modern warfare from those traditional forms that still allow for male solidarity within the army, the additional control necessary for reliable interpretation would be available despite the inevitable case loss stemming from lack of data.

Change in articulation level could not be directly coded either, but the cumulative characteristic of this variable permits inferences as to change over time. The basis for these inferences is as follows: Given a cross-tabulation of degree of articulation with decline in ceremonies, one may expect the greatest decline to occur in the upper levels. This is so because over time these communities have moved from lower levels to their present articulation level.

But does one know that this sequence actually occurred? Perhaps the community has always functioned at that level. Or perhaps it did not go through those particular steps. Or perhaps it declined from a higher level. The logic of cumulative scales permits us to say, however, that these alternatives are improbable. If the 54 communities had taken different routes to arrive at their present articulation level, the characteristics of their change would have shown up as scale error. A scale would simply not have been possible. While it is possible that a community could be created containing the total range of attributes required by the scale and thus not show up as an error case, such an exception would be obvious; in any event this has not happened with these particular villages. It is equally improbable, in an era when modernization is spreading rather than receding, that a village has attained a higher level and then dropped down. Thus, a community's articulation level does imply earlier development over time and may be compared with direct evidence of change in other aspects of structure. Table 32 gives the pertinent data.

TABLE 32.   **Relationship of Decline in Initiation Ceremonies to Community-Nation Articulation Level**

	Local autonomy (steps 1-3)	*Representative contact (steps 4-8)*	*Urban inter-penetration (steps 9-10)*
Evidence of decline in male initiation ceremonies	9	18	30
Total cases	(11)	(22)	(20)
Evidence of decline in female initiation ceremonies	9	10	40
Total cases	(11)	(21)	(20)

That the percentage of male and female initiation ceremonies showing some decline is greater in the modernized communities than in those of medium articulation supports the hypotheses that articulation weakens solidarity and that solidarity is related to degree of dramatization. Moreover, the difference between the male and female proportions at different articulation levels throws additional light on changes in the sex-related structures. On the face of it, the solidary family is most vulnerable to modernization, for 40 per cent of the communities show female initiation decline at levels 9 and 10. But another interpretation is possible if one compares the percentages at middle and upper articulation levels for each sex. Male initiation shows greater attenuation in the middle levels, and much of the change is completed by the upper levels. Female initiation is resistant to change in the middle levels and then erodes more rapidly in the upper levels. Thus, instead of being more vulnerable to modernization, its relative lack of decline until upper articulation levels are reached is more an indication of its holding power even under changing conditions. So interpreted, these data align with the general picture of the more widely adaptable solidary family suggested by the greater frequency of its occurrence, most especially in the lowest and highest articulation levels, where male solidarity tends not to occur.

A Restudy of a Bifurcated Society: Manus

Of the few but remarkable restudies made in recent years by anthropologists, the investigation by Margaret Mead (1961) of a New Guinea village stands out as especially relevant to the present research. When first studied in 1928, the village of Peri maintained both male and female initiation ceremonies and, as the following analysis will show, was a bifurcated society in all respects. But by 1953, when Mead returned, the ceremonies had died out. Had male and female solidarity also faded? And did the village articulate with modern society according to the hypotheses that this study has explored on a cross-cultural basis?

Old Peri, as the 1928 village is distinguished, was something of a Pacific Venice because all its houses were built over the water on stilts and the 210 inhabitants were as well adapted to canoe travel and swimming as other groups are to terrestial activity. The subsistence base, in 1953 as in 1928, was fishing, although wage work on plantations and in New Guinea towns increased after the first period of study. By 1953 the villagers had moved to the shore of the lagoon and rebuilt their community according to the strict rectilinear pattern of American military installations. Twenty-five years earlier Peri had been "an aggregate of loosely organized paternal exogamous clans, all bound together by mutual economic obligations incurred through marriages between their members, obligations which [were] enforced by the spirits of the dead acting through mediums" (1959:176). By 1953 it had the beginnings of a formal village council and more explicit rules of conduct. According to Mead, the main external determinants of change came when World War II brought Japanese regimentation and then American abundance. A second event during the 25-year interval was the influence of a native leader named Paliau, who organized one of the religious and nationalistic movements that have so often developed in the Pacific Islands.

Despite Mead's emphasis on the psychological and processual aspects of her materials, her account includes the basic data required for assessing the community in terms of the variables of this study. As the summary in Table 33 (p. 134-5) indicates, the Manus maintained a bifurcated society in 1928 despite the prohibition of local warfare and the encroachments of civilization. Although the fishing economy did not facilitate the collective subsistence activity found in other bifurcated communities, the account indicates clearly that men and women nonetheless formed separate community networks. Perhaps the small size of the village and the frequent coordination of effort among the various families made it possible to maintain their taut social structure, characterized by Mead as "puritanical." What is undeniable, however, is that male solidarity existed; it was focused in the exclusive masculine activities that took place on a small island some distance from the village. There the men constructed canoes and fish traps and frequented the club house that formerly housed the prostitutes kept by the young men.

The family also, although not enlarged by a great many additional nuclear families, was nonetheless solidary according to the criteria used in this study. The household guardians or ancestors symbolized the unity of the household group; these spirits were also associated with the trading carried on by Manus families. Perhaps the demands and rewards of maintaining a place in the commercial network were crucial preconditions of the cohesive family structure. At any rate there was a strict separation of the adults within the household organization; the sexes slept apart, and the women were expected to be deferential, hard working, and seclusive about sex. In later life women were important in their husbands' trading ventures, an activity which tended to equalize their status; and, as in all societies, they had their informal comeback. Yet it can hardly be said that the village of Peri, as of 1928, allowed women much latitude.

The Manus nuclear family was embedded in a patrilocal clan organization, and marriage was more a contract between families than between individuals. The young couple's position was quite unsettled until the wife bore her first child; and if this was long in coming, she could attempt to return to her own family. Even after the child was born, the young couple led a marginal existence "skulking about the back doors of their rich relatives' houses," as Mead expresses the particular Manus variation on a theme as old as the extended family.

This community and family solidarity was accompanied by semielaborate initiation ceremonies and a maximally elaborate ritual recognition of parenthood. Thus, in main outline, Manus culture, as represented by the village of Peri, in 1928 conformed to the theoretical expectations for bifurcated societies. As civilization pressed in upon it, however, changing the subsistence pattern and forcing the community to move to a new site on the beach, its social structure shifted markedly and the recognition of sex role was divested of drama.

Mead's interpretation of these changes contrasts with one implied by this research. For her, the relatively smooth shift of structure experienced by the Manus came about through the conjunction of two sets of factors: "We have seen how in the Manus cultural character we had found a point of leverage for change in the discontinuity between the happy comradeship of childhood and adolescence and the realities of adult life, but a point which without a changed external situation might never have been used" (1961:184). She hypothesizes that discontinuous socialization, such as the Manus—and Americans—undergo, predisposes them to social change in the direction already taken by Americans. But this change cannot occur unless there is exposure to such a modernized culture pattern, and this, she feels, is unpredictable. This appeal to the internal themes of the culture, as initiated in the socialization process, in combination with the fortuitous rush of history, is an old one in American anthropology and appeals to common sense. It coincides with the tendency of Americans to interpret their own history as the domination of the unharnessed resources and events of the New World by the pioneer spirit.

But can we now maintain so simple an interpretation? When the

TABLE 33. **Selected Aspects of Social Structure: Peri, 1928, 1953**[*]

Aspect of structure	1928	1953
1. Subsistence base	Fishing and gathering of sea life, some pigs kept on shore. Beginnings of wage work for younger men. Trading.	Fishing, gathering, and pigs, but wage work more prevalent. Considerable experience with such work during war. Trading.
2. Articulation level	Step 6: Full-time bureaucrats. Missionaries not yet active in village. One error because the village has no public structure.	Step 9: Formal education for both sexes, although rudimentary. No errors.
3. Sexual division of labor	No village-wide collective work by either sex, but a sharp division of work is maintained.	Continued absence of collective subsistence work, but now intersex cooperation in fishing.
4. Family solidarity	Monogamous households, but frequent addition of nuclear families of children, and occasionally of more wives. Each household has guardian spirit and lineage symbolization that is focused on most recently deceased ancestor. Husband and wife sleep on opposite sides of house.	Monogamous, independent households with occasional additional relatives, usually single. No evidence of a norm of household separation or symbolization of unity.
5. Male solidarity	Men have exclusive use of a small island, where they build canoes and fish traps, but former male religious activity connected with the island is dying out.	No village-wide male solidarity. The role of the island as a center of male activity has faded.

[*] Mead 1959, 1961.

TABLE 33. (Continued)

Aspect of structure	1928	1953
6. Warfare	Local wars involving head-hunting prohibited by colonial authorities about 1900.	No warfare. Natives did not participate officially in World War II, which swept through the area.
7. Male initiation	Step 3: Ear-piercing, ceremonial dress, boy goes to island for blessing. No hazing. Age 12-16. Typically one boy at time. Festivities last several days and involve bisexual group larger than family. But wage work in other places is interfering.	No dramatic initiation. Most boys have wage work experience.
8. Female initiation	Step 3: Ceremony for individual girl at first menstruation, involving seclusion, ceremonial chasing by grandmother, and feasting of bisexual group larger than family. Lasts a week or so.	Apparently none.
9. Recognition of parenthood	Step 5 elaboration, but no data for step 3. Concern over newborn, ritual behavior of mother during pregnancy and of father after birth, and isolation of mother and child for a period after birth.	Probably informal only. Definitely no ritual concern over newborn or isolation of mother after childbirth, but data lacking on other steps.

spread of civilization is characterized particularistically as the coming of the American army and as the rise of a regional leader, then it does seem quite lacking in regularity. But when coded as steps in the scale of articulation, it appears quite orderly, and we are prompted to say that Westernization would have come anyway—as indeed it has in Melanesia in places that escaped the war and in which no native leader arose to excite the population.

And once doubt is raised on the conceptualization of external factors, an analogous question may be raised about the socialization determinant. For Mead, it is not the particular practices but the discontinuity between childhood and the adult situation that is predisposing. "Looking at the Manus in 1928-29, one could note the discrepancy between childhood and adulthood, the sullen misery of the young people as they met the demands of the adult world, and one could note the counterparts in the United States in young people who found the world to be something different from what they had been led to expect" (1961:139). Her observation of Manus development makes sense in terms of the highly institutionalized family and community, which has no place for any but disciplined adults. The same discontinuity has often been noted in primitive societies. But the reference to the United States, where male and female solidarity are generally not strong, is disconcerting. If societies as apparently different as the United States and Manus are seen as predisposing toward change, it is difficult to imagine what type of society is not.

When one thinks of the typical traditional and unchanging community, where the son regularly learns to take his father's place, one finds oneself thinking of folk communities like Manus that maintain a definite separation between the adult's world and the child's. It seems that the very societies that are noteworthy for their tendency not to change have socialization patterns that, according to Mead, predispose them toward change. Of course, one might argue that predisposition is only that, and that Western contact is required. But few societies have not been minimally Westernized by now. The war that Mead cites in the case of Manus was not fought on every island, but it is doubtful that many places did not hear the roar.

Without pursuing additional complexities, is there not a simpler alternative? Can we not say that communities with male and female solidarity will tend to modernize simply because it is these communities that have generally reached the middle levels of articulation and are ready to move on to the next? Granted that the absence of an organized national or colonial structure sets an upper limit on articulation, it is not necessary to seek the predisposing factor in the socialization pattern of children. Socialization may determine some of the later personality trends in the individual, but it is a fallacy to leap from individual determinants to the social structure of the community. Rather, the preconditions for change are part of the going social organization, and that organization, let it be emphasized, is maintained by adults. If these adults have developed or accepted a mode of social control that is reliable, and if they are engaged in commercial and social relations with other communities, then they will move on to more complex ways of articulating with the modern world. If the American army moves by or a regional leader comes with a new ideology, these or equivalent events will extend the level of community articulation. More precisely, the community members will publicly discriminate new categories of social meaning, and these new categories will allow them to comprehend and to interact with the larger modernized structures around them. That is what articulation implies.

Within the theoretical framework of this study, one would interpret the discontinuous socialization practices of the Manus as simply another way of describing the social distance between solidary adults and their children. One would also reject the equating of Manus and American society with regard to the discontinuity of socialization. However, it is to the distinct credit of *New Lives for Old* that it provides the basis for alternative interpretations while offering and supporting its own. Actually, the materials are far more intricate than can be indicated in this brief discussion. It should not be necessary to add that no decision can be reached regarding the validity of the two interpretations; only a differential test of a sort unlikely to be designed for some years could encompass the inherent complexities.

Solidarity and Articulation
in Theoretical Perspective

At the theoretical level, the analysis of social change presented in this chapter takes the form of an interplay between articulation and solidarity. The former concept has been defined as the degree to which the members of a community publicly discriminate different areas of social meaning. In practice this differentiation is identified by the different "institutions" of the community, and, indirectly, that is what the scale of articulation measures. However, it also measures the external transactions that the community has with the wider society, and the label "articulation" calls attention to this fact more than the otherwise acceptable term "differentiation." Male solidarity, in contrast, was defined as the degree to which the men of the community hold a unified, stable, or crystallized group image. Solidarity is the degree of synthesis of differentiated social meanings. Perhaps solidarity may be considered the degree to which the various sectors of social meaning held by a group implicate one another. A familiar example in modern times is the nationalistic country in which nearly every aspect of life is interpreted from the point of view of the interests of the state.

Although solidarity was indexed for only one part of the membership of the community, the concept was extended to the whole community on the argument that the scale of solidarity could be so interpreted. That is, male solidarity was redefined as community solidarity, the implication being that women typically share the image of the group maintained by the men. Thus, articulation and solidarity constitute two group-wide dimensions of organization, each of which is always present to some degree in all social systems.

Although it is difficult to relate these two concepts precisely to the great flow of ideas that the past century of sociological thought has bequeathed, there are a number of points of articulation. First and foremost, two separate variables, each with its two poles, are proposed instead of the usual one-dimensional characterization implied by such concepts as folk-urban, *Gemeinschaft-Gesellschaft*, sacred-secular, mechanical-organic, or traditional-modern. An example will make this usage clear. For empirical illustration of the folk end of his folk-urban continuum, Redfield (1941) cites the village of Tusik in Quintana Roo. As it turns out, this village is rather unusual. When the Mexican Army reasserted government control of the territory in 1901, the native communities retreated into the bush, where they developed a strong defensive position. They maintained a local military organization along with the typical native religious interpenetration of village life. Although the Indians sold chicle, hogs, and poultry to traveling merchants, they used American and British currency and distrusted and despised Mexican money. In general they maintained a suspiciousness toward outsiders of such intensity that

Villa Rojas, who did the field work in the village, had to enter in the guise of a traveling merchant.

Now, it is not denied that this community is differentiated less than the others described by Redfield. The point is that something more is involved. Tusik is an "encysted" community; over and above its low level of articulation, it maintains a strong community-wide solidarity. This mixing up of what from the point of view of this study are two separate dimensions is further reflected in Redfield's conceptual definitions of his three basic variables. His concepts of individualization and secularization seem quite consistent with the articulation variable, which is equivalent to differentiation. But the "organization of culture," defined as "the extent to which the society may be described in terms of a single—only one—organized body of conventional understanding" (1941:346) seems to emphasize the solidarity factor. Actually, the concepts of solidarity and differentiation are more in line with recent conceptual trends than with those of the past. The notions of "adaptation" and "integration," as used by Parsons and Bales (Bales 1943), or the "complexity" and "order" dimensions that Wallace (1961b:143ff.) discusses seem roughly cognate.

A second feature of these concepts of solidarity and differentiation is that they are content-free and refer to the same level of data. That is, in contrast to a pair like sacred-secular or even *Gemeinschaft-Gesellschaft*, solidarity and differentiation are less bound to the content of the data. Almost any human product may be analyzed from the point of view of its differentiation or unity of meaning, in contrast to the somewhat greater restriction to the ritual or rational or emotional content required by other concepts. Insofar as concepts are formal, they have a better chance of cross-cultural applicability than those that are content- and therefore culture-bound. Another advantage is that both concepts apply to the conventional meanings held by a group. This is not true of pairs like "functional" versus "cultural" integration, or adaptation and morale. Hopefully, such alignment of both concepts to the same empirical point of reference will help to avoid confusion.

A weakness of these concepts, at least in the present study, is that the indices are indirect. Both scales use gross organizational patterns for measuring what ultimately is a pattern of ideas. It is assumed that there is no fundamental distinction between the institutionalized interaction used in the scales and the conventional meanings that are aspects of such organization, but it would be useful to be able to show empirically that such is the case.

One immediately senses a certain antithesis between these two dimensions of solidarity and differentiation. It is almost a common-sense hypothesis that the one increases at the expense of the other, and it is easy to think of social movements that sacrifice all diversity to the "cause" or of organizations so differentiated that they achieve unity only in the characteristics of a leader or his office. This study supports the antithesis up to a point, with the finding of a curvilinear relationship between the two. It is argued that community-wide solidarity, by and large, is infrequent in either pluralistic or nomadic societies. Said positively, the peasant level of subsistence and organization, which involves a limited contact with the larger national structure, is a favorable environment for the rather rigid institutionalization that characterizes male solidarity. It is understood that under certain conditions, chiefly those of warfare, both nomadic and modern societies develop an over-all cohesion that should show up at the community level.

The curvilinear relationship has another side, however. Although the typical route to increased articulation is by way of the preceding steps without any special elaboration of solidarity, the latter development also leads toward greater articulation. Although solidary communities reduce some of their ties with other groups, they increase others, especially alliances for war and certain transactions involving subsistence activity. Moreover, the greater flexibility of movement that typically goes with autonomous organization gives such communities a comparative advantage that may in time bring them into new relationships with the national structure, opening the way for greater articulation. In a word, solidarity may be the organizational form most useful in breaking through the many development "ceilings" that tend to form in all societies.

Summary

This chapter brings together two lines of research embodied in the previous chapters by combining male and female solidarity into a typology. In order to do this, male solidarity is redefined as community solidarity, as in Chapter 6 female solidarity was redefined as family solidarity. Thus, the typology is one of the interrelations of family and community.

These are analyzed against levels of articulation and related factors. Communities having neither community nor family solidarity tend to be modernized, while communities with only one type of solidarity seem to reflect ecologically specialized, but traditional, environments. Like the latter communities, those with both types of solidarity fall in the middle ranges of articulation, but unlike them, they seem to reflect a situation of separate but intercommunicating large family units often associated with a transition to modern status.

The relationship between social change and solidarity is considered both empirically, by analysis of the decline of initiation ceremonies and through a case study of a New Guinea village at two points in time, and theoretically, in terms of the conceptual status of the dimensions of solidarity and articulation.

8. Reconsiderations: Functionalism, Dramatization, and the Sociogenic-Psychogenic Dialogue

In one interpretation of scientific enterprise, the suggestions emerging from an investigation, even though unproved by the available evidence, are the real climax of a study. Substantive results come and go, but heuristic ideas, whether methodological or conceptual, are the veins that continue to be worked. Thus, there is always the final question: is this line of thought worth continuing? While what follows will raise doubts about the functional format in which this study is embedded, the concept of dramatization seems to hold many new possibilities.

Functional Equivalents and Alternatives

Many recent analyses of functionalism have emphasized the role of functional equivalents or alternatives. Examples of this phenomenon are many: magic is a substitute for rational knowledge, agoraphobia for claustrophobia, the political machine for democratic representation; and marrying sisters, appointing a head wife, or maintaining separate households are all ways of reducing domestic discord in polygynous families. For these instances the term "equivalents" should be used. There is no complex interrelationship between the items; either will serve as well. The term "alternatives" may be reserved for those customs, to be discussed later, in which two factors bear a compensatory relationship to each other.

Functional theorists assume that social systems constantly exhibit such equivalences. Therefore, if a theory is to be true to nature, it must make a place for the interchangeability of customs. More generally, all open systems are assumed to develop multiple ways of adapting to their changing environments. This same point has been made in another way by Merton (1957:36) when he points out that the idea of functional equivalents is a more adequate conception than that of functional indispensability. To assume the latter requires one to assert that all customs, from men's extra coat buttons to the many superstitions held by scientifically trained people, are indispensable to the functioning of the community. It is easier to believe that some one of a cluster of interchangeable beliefs may be necessary for the functioning of a given social structure.

This study has turned up a number of functional equivalents. Chapter 4 treated collective male subsistence work and local warfare as variants of male solidarity. Collective male work, in turn, was a composite of collective hunting, fishing, and herding of large animals, each taken as interchangeable with the others. Again, the broadly organized male solidarity indexed by the presence of a Moslem mosque seemed equivalent to the segmented male solidarity indicated by multiple men's houses. Another equivalence was polygyny and an extended family composed of a number of nuclear units; both customs provide many women for the domestic unit.

But this list gives rise to two objections. Are not most of these simply equivalent indicators? Certainly they were used as such. When separate analysis indicated that herding gave the same results as collective hunting or fishing, they were combined. In the different economies those modes of exploitation represent equivalent adaptations, but as indices of male communication they are the same. Unless some distinction is made between equivalent indicators and equivalent adaptations, a whole range of examples must be relegated to the category of semantic problems. One solution might be to agree that functional substitutes must be conceptually distinct. Thus, segmented and generalized types of male solidarity seem to exhibit sufficient difference to justify separate categorization (even though they were not so treated in this research). Analogously, initiation ceremonies are different from a shift of the adolescent's sleeping quarters by virtue of the greater ritualization of the former.

But the introduction of the requirement of conceptual distinctness for functional equivalents highlights another objection. If two customs quite often occur together, as do male initiation and shift of sleeping quarters, should they be considered functional substitutes? Are they not better termed "functional supplements"? Admittedly, restricting the term "equivalents" to customs that are mutually exclusive greatly reduces the number of instances to be found, but it might improve the precision of this framework. It would eliminate, for instance, the often claimed substitutability of magic and cognitive knowledge because these frequently exist together. Of course, it might be possible to find particular customs that stand in an either/or relationship, but the empirical problem seems formidable.

Further complicating the picture is a restriction mentioned by Hempel (1959:285). The conditions under which a substitution may occur must be rigorously specified. Otherwise, one can claim that the presence of a substitute so changes the nature of the system that the functional equivalents are no longer comparable—and thereby define the problem out of existence. On the other hand, some instances of major system-change seem justified. Thus, Chapter 1 argued that the initiation ceremonies characteristic of many subgroups of complex societies are not equivalent to the community-wide customs of primitive groups because they involve a shift from a community to a national unit of analysis. But it is a nice problem to draw the line. If the range of structural variation is too narrow, then functional equivalents become impossible. If it is too wide, one excludes the real possibility of structural differences or levels and denies a significant kind of social change. This problem has usually been discussed in connection with the "principle of limited possibilities," but the methodological ground rules are still quite vague.

All these problems converge in the one area where functional equivalence should be clearest, in the customs of initiation ceremonies themselves. It was expected that the myriad customs of initiation would be highly interchangeable. And to some extent they are. Within scale steps, many items operate in the same way. Thus, a new name, new clothing, a gift, or a festive gathering all qualify as minimal social attention. But this type of interchangeability is open to the interpretation suggested above, that the items are simply alternate indicators. All index the single concept of minimal social attention. Conceptual distinctness is given by the several steps in the scale: individualized attention, social response, and so forth. But the fact that they are steps in a scale is clear evidence that they are not equivalents. Cumulation is a principle quite different from functional substitution.

The usefulness of the principle of functional equivalence is further undermined when it is recalled that the *degree* of solidarity is associated with the *degree* of dramatization. That is, each step is predictable—just the opposite from the unpredictability that Hempel says holds for the items within a given step and that led him to characterize functional analysis as weak causal analysis. And the possibility of predicting a few scale steps suggests that more refined analysis would enable us to predict many more. One is prompted to wonder whether strong causal analysis is not possible after all. At any rate, the pessimistic character of Hempel's analysis is exposed.

There is, however, a different conception of this problem that may supersede the somewhat static notion of equivalence. In a welcome contribution to the literature, Francesca Cancian (1960) has shown the relevance to sociology of Nagel's (1957:247-83) formulation of functionalism. The third element in her definition of a functional system is pertinent: "there are certain limits in the variation of the values of state coordinates such that variation within the limits will be followed by a compensating variation of other state coordinates, resulting in the maintenance of G" (Cancian 1960:821). Thus, at least two variables in a compensatory relationship are required, either one of which can maintain a given state of the system. In the example she takes from Bales's work on small groups, G is the resolution of the group's task or problem, and the functional alternatives are task-oriented and emotionally supportive activity. At any one time one or the other of these variables may be dominant, but if the dominant variable moves up to its limit, the other comes into play to compensate for the potential disruption of the system. If a group has a hard-driving, task-oriented leader, he may move everyone toward greater productivity for a time, but at some point someone else will have to do something about the increasing number of complaints and general low morale. Thus, a frequent outcome would be a cyclical course for any one variable.

Applying this construction to initiation ceremonies, one must imagine some kind of activity that stands in a compensatory relationship to dramatization so that solidarity is always maintained at a given level. It is not obvious what this activity might be, but one can sup-

pose, analogizing from television commercials, that too much dramatization would lead to a demand for some real demonstration of merit.
No matter how loyal the initiates are to the beliefs of the men, they
would not be much good on a head-hunting expedition if they did
not know how to fight. This formulation makes initiation ceremonies
the independent variable and solidarity the consequence. A further
implication is that for any given cross-tabulation of initiation dramatization and solidarity, the association may vary all the way from zero
to one, depending upon the point in the cycle that is tapped. On the
other hand, if the finding is that a given degree of solidarity is always
matched with a particular level of dramatization, we may conclude
that no compensatory variable is operating. Thus, the result presented
in Table 12 of Chapter 4 (p. 75) seems sufficient to rule out a functional alternative of this type.

If this is so, the question is again raised: is functional analysis necessary? It may be that true functional alternatives are fairly rare or
that they are apparent only with precise experimental techniques.
Clear demonstration of functional alternation seems to require a time
study so that the cyclical nature of the relationship is revealed. Such
systematic observation is probably not possible with ethnographic
data. And if these phenomena are rare to begin with, it may be convenient to avoid the complexities of the functional framework and to
use the more straightforward pattern of causal, albeit multivariate,
analysis from the start.

Survival and Termination of Social Systems

In the latter part of his book *The Human Group*, George Homans,
taking a turn at functional methodology, stirs up in the course of a
few pages most of the problems this study has encountered in attempt-
ing to pin down empirically a second tenet of the framework: the absence of a custom that is functionally necessary leads to the failure
of the system. Homans comments as follows:

> In the second place, the meaning of *survival* or *continuity* is not always
> clear. . . . [The social anthropologist] is not in the position of a biolo-
> gist in a laboratory, experimenting with a cat's nervous system in
> order to determine what changes impair its "survival value." . . . If

we turn to history for help, it is astonishing how few societies have failed to survive. No doubt some primitive societies have disappeared, and all their members have died out, like the last of the Mohicans. But by far the most usual situation resembles the decline and fall of the Roman Empire. What fell then was not a society but a governmental organization. . . . The meaning of social survival can be made much more precise for small units and organizations within a society than for the society itself . . . [1951:269-70].

Given all these problems, it would seem unwise to attempt an empirical specification of the degree of persistence or survival, but there is a pressing methodological reason for at least exploring the problem. If functional analysis is correct in asserting that under certain conditions a system does not survive without certain classes of customs, then many deviant cases might be explained by measuring the level of functioning. For instance, the occurrence of a number of instances of male solidarity without the predicted dramatization of status might make sense if it could be shown that the society or the male organization itself was at a low ebb and on the way to extinction. Such analysis might be particularly pertinent when the data come from one of the last surviving members of a society or from a highly acculturated group. Perhaps the case of the Navaho, whose sweat houses still have enough religious overtones to require that they be coded as instances of male solidarity, is an example. They do not have initiations, but of course they do not have much solidarity either.

However, the thinking during the beginning phases of this research was cruder than the foregoing discussion would suggest. The first attempts to index disintegration took the whole community as a unit. The starting point of the pilot investigation was the framework of Aberle *et al.* (1950), who propose four types of societal termination: (a) biological extinction or dispersion of the members, (b) apathy, (c) the war of all against all, and (d) the absorption of the society by another. Of course, in practice all these pathologies converge, and the most obvious outcome, as Homans says, is that a community is assimilated, either as a unit or family by family, into another society.

But the pilot study's attempt to go beyond the anthropologist's implicit index of survival (i.e., that the community existed, at least in the minds of old people, at the time of the interviews) produced some disconcerting difficulties. For instance, how is a decline of population to be interpreted? Is it the route to termination, or is it simply a redistribution of the population? Granted that migration implies the termination of the particular community under study, is the meaning of termination the same for these different kinds of biological extinction—decimation by disease, say, versus migration to a large city? And if the community has a population that is rapidly expanding, interpretation is equally difficult. Is a "population explosion" an adequate index of survival, particularly when the organization of the society may be disintegrating under the resulting pressure?

Unfortunately it is no help to turn to the other three types of termination, because the available empirical indicators seem equally uninterpretable. Is the apathy that may occur during a social revolution necessarily an indicator of community weakness? An important question is the segment of the population that is apathetic. Similarly, assimilation has many meanings, from conquest to participation in the benefits of an advanced society. It is always possible, of course, that more precise indicators will be contrived and these ambiguities dissolved, but it is doubtful whether cross-cultural data will take us that far.

Perhaps the fundamental question raised by these empirical snarls is simply: what do we mean by a society or a community? Formal definitions are of course available, and that proposed by Aberle *et al.*[1] is well worked out. But of more relevance to functional analysis are the attempts, through a list of "requisites" or "basic needs," to specify the components without which a social system has no meaning. Such "conditions without which" are usually given potential empirical status, but it is also possible to interpret them simply as aspects of the concept. In fact, even brief consideration suffices to show that it is impossible to take them otherwise. The pattern of analysis of Aberle *et al.* is to say that the absence of customs serving a postulated requisite leads to one or more of the four modes of termination. Thus, no society can survive without "shared cognitive orientations." But is such a community even imaginable? It is unnecessary to move through a ponderous mental sequence, imagining first that a community with-

[1] Society is defined as "a group of human beings sharing a self-sufficient system of action which is capable of existing longer than the life-span of an individual, the group being recruited at least in part by the the sexual reproduction of the members" (Aberle *et al.* 1950:101).

out shared cognitive orientations would not be able to cooperate for food production, then that it develops internal conflicts and apathy, and finally that it is absorbed by a group that does have shared cognitive orientations. Is it not sufficient to say that a community, by definition, must have shared cognitive orientations?

If lists of prerequisites are taken simply as a way of specifying the social scientist's conception of society, they raise the problem of distinguishing among them. The various needs are so ill-defined that they give little guidance to empirical efforts. Aspects like "shared cognitive orientations," "shared, articulated set of goals," and "normative regulation of means" tend to fade into one another. Nonetheless, this mode of elaborating the meaning of our definition of society has one clear advantage over some other ways in that it focuses attention on the group-level character of the phenomenon. It suggests the answer to a question that Homans obviously meant as a conversation-stopper: "But surely the two things are not independent: group survival is inconceivable without some degree of satisfaction of individual needs" (1951:268). On the contrary, if a group is defined by the presence of systematic relationships of needs, sentiments, and the like, then it is perfectly possible to think about the survival of the pattern of relationships without once referring to individual needs. Homans' own work demonstrates that this can be done, and everyone does it when he sees a group persisting despite a turnover in membership.

Perhaps one empirical outcome of the study of community survival deserves mention. In coding the state of community functioning, it became a rule of thumb to consider the group as "existing," at least at a minimal level, if there is evidence that the members hold a unified definition of their situation. The cross-cultural data did not permit reliable coding of the organization of meanings, but it was generally possible to reject the scraps of remembered culture that often pass for an account of a social group, or to decide that the conventional meanings held in a given community are so assimilated into a larger system that the community could not be considered an independent unit for research purposes. Although the organization of conventional meanings is a part of most definitions of community, this element becomes especially useful in the investigation as soon as one pays attention to the organization and not the particular meanings. When a group of people seem to have an over-all conception of what they are doing, regardless of the content of their activity, it is possible to accept them as a unit and go on with the empirical operations. Their designation as a village, a family, or a men's group depends, of course, on other refining attributes.

As unsuccessful as the study of survival and termination generally was, it may have had one useful outcome in that it led to the substitution of "level of solidarity" for conceptions like "likelihood of termination." In other words, the research paid less attention to the decline of social groups, an idea that is useful only for extreme cases anyway, and more to the level of functioning. As interpreted by the scale, level of functioning is synonymous with degree of solidarity, and this measure in turn may be considered equivalent to the degree to which a social system is a going system. If this solution to the "survival problem" withstands critical scrutiny, it will have as its principal virtue the fact that it is empirically feasible.

Problems of the Dramaturgical Frame of Reference

This study was initially conceptualized in Durkheimian terms, in what might be called a "solidarity" framework. Although the investigation did not abandon this emphasis—the hypothesis always took solidarity as the independent variable—the emphasis did shift to the extent that the dramaturgical approach of the sort that Kenneth Burke (1954, 1962) and his followers have experimented with covers the ground more adequately. Some of the conceptual problems inherent in this viewpoint merit more discussion.

A key question is the nature of dramatization. Chapter 1 recognized that it is a form of social communication, but otherwise much was taken for granted. Actually, a dictionary definition, such as the first chapter depended upon, has drawbacks. To emphasize the reaction of the audience is at best to introduce considerable indirection into the measurement problem. This is particularly true when the audience reaction is covert. Applause meters are not the most adequate measure of an enactment so impressive that one sees the world differently from that time forward. Similarly, to emphasize the "intrinsic" qualities of gestures, artifacts, and words is to sidestep the basic problem. As Durkheim reminded us, there is nothing obviously intrinsic in sign-vehicles; the whole range of utterances and objects is available to serve as symbol carriers. Rather, the problem of definition must be met in the communication itself. Is there no way to describe the phenomenon in its own terms? In his discussion of dramatic realization, Goffman mentions the temporal distribution of the stimuli, the substitution of visible for invisible activity, and the arrangement of the symbols:

> . . . Thus, if a baseball umpire is to give the impression that he is sure of his judgment, he must forego the moment of thought which might make him sure of his judgment; he must give an instantaneous decision so that the audience will be sure that he is sure of his judgment [1959:30].

> . . . Undertakers must therefore charge a great deal for their highly visible product—a coffin that has been transformed into a casket—because many of the other costs of conducting a funeral are ones that cannot be readily dramatized [1959:32].

> . . . Thus, to furnish a house so that it will express simple, quiet dignity, the householder may have to race to auction sales, haggle with antique dealers, and doggedly canvass all the local shops for proper wallpaper and curtain materials [1959:32].

Perhaps these and other characteristics of dramatic communication may be summarized by defining it as a combination of symbols such that one part of the message articulates with other parts so that the probability of interpreting it in a certain way is sharply increased. Thus, political slogans, wrapping paper, or appearing in a tight red dress all have in common the manipulation of symbols so that some aspects of the message stand out over others. In contrast to scientific communication, which attempts to find a hypothesis that fits a situation, dramatization creates a situation that predetermines the hypothesis. Clearly, hypotheses must be readily available, and the symbols must have acquired certain "loadings." Dramatic effort builds on the available understandings but adds to them a particular form of organization. Happily, words may be infinitely combined to achieve dramatic qualities, and nonverbal symbols seem to have the same potentiality.

Although the ethnographies do not tell us so, it must be assumed that verbal communication is as important in primitive ceremonials as it is in modern ritual. Like archeology, cross-cultural indices must utilize gross facts to index what is more directly a tissue of meanings attached to sound patterns. But nothing we know about the human use of language suggests that the cultures studied by anthropologists are limited in their use of verbal symbolism. However, the emphasis on overt activity that is built into the scale of dramatization may reflect a true characteristic of such communication. The meanings conveyed are typically diffuse. The hypothesis or image conveyed by the generalized ritual acts usually concerns general values or attitudes.

Of course, one may question this generalization by suggesting that the nature of the sign-vehicles is such that precise meanings are not denotable. But the converse hypothesis, that dramatic communication typically requires the use of somewhat gross sign-vehicles, is equally tenable. Stimuli that vary greatly in intensity but are restricted in complexity make good carriers of dramatic communication. Thus pain, wailing, or similar human sounds; generalized color, including black and white; or the effects of drugs, intoxicants, or fatigue are frequent media for dramatic effects. So are simple gestures and standardized sayings. Admittedly, the flexibility of language, like a digital computor, may be harnessed for such communicative work. The speeches in plays interweave and culminate to achieve an effect not contained in any one. Similarly, the total color scheme of a room is the determinant of the mood it creates. But even here complexity works toward a certain simplicity of effect.

The hypothesized relationship between type of sign-vehicle and dramatic communication clarifies a problem that has a long history in social thought. What is the relationship between the form and the content of a communication? On the one hand we have the opinion of linguists and psychologists that symbols are entirely conventional. Moreover, the variation in the content and the impact of particular situations seems so great as to preclude a test of cross-cultural hypotheses that must assume equivalence of meaning. And yet, certain activities—like fighting—have an apparent panhuman meaning, and other activities—like hazing—appear at only one end of the dramatization scale. One interpretation of these apparent regularities turns on the nature of the sign-vehicles involved. There are many ways to communicate hostility, but physical attack, because it is limited in complexity but varies widely in intensity, may be a frequently and universally used sign-vehicle. The four items of Whiting's index of initiation may admit of a similar interpretation. Hazing, genital operations, separation from one's social group, and seclusion all make prominent use of the intensity principle. Thus one obtains an empirical result in some cases because a given sign-vehicle may be associated with a near-universal meaning; in other cases the homogeneity of the behavioral sign-vehicles introduces an element of spuriousness with respect to hypotheses about the meaning of situations.

The role of dramatization as a communication strategy is further clarified by contrasting it to other possible strategies. Following Goffman's proposals, we may consider "idealization," "mystification," and "misrepresentation." Goffman explains the first as a person's tendency "to incorporate and exemplify the officially accredited values of the society, more so, in fact, than does his behavior as a whole" (1959:35). The efforts of socially mobile persons provide the type case for individuals, but the process is also apparent in groups, as among those Indian castes that have "Sanskritized" their ritual or the many business concerns that hire "scientists" as window-dressing. In formal terms, symbols typically associated with another style of life are appropriated for at least temporary use. The requirement that such symbols be officially credited or "higher" in some sense seems unnecessary. At any rate the meaning of these terms becomes quite vague in cases where a rich man assumes the humble garb and way of life of the poor or a dentist organizes his professional work along "ideal" commercial lines.

Mystification is the communication strategy that restricts the kind and amount of information available to an audience. The information that is withheld is usually of the everyday sort that most people do not bother to control, but it becomes significant to high-status people who must not appear to be ordinary. "Familiarity breeds contempt" is, of course, the folk formulation of this rule of impression management, and the standard stratagem is the maintenance of social distance.

The third strategy, misrepresentation, may be poorly named. As Goffman himself makes clear, the connotation of falsification that this term carries is not conceptually useful. We do not consider a high-

status person who travels incognito as misrepresenting himself, no
are we ordinarily outraged at white lies, the exemplary dress and
behavior of serious job-seekers, or the fact that towns in tropical areas
may be sprayed with insecticides before an important visitor arrives
What is sociologically crucial is the lack of congruence between one
part of the communication and the rest, a contrast which, as Goffman
points out, makes such performances subject to disruption.

There are a number of other communication strategies that might
be mentioned: formalization, the use of irony or satire, or the "pa
rochialization" and "universalization" that Redfield discusses (1956:
94-96). The last mode of communication, which seems similar to
Parsons' "universalistic" or Weber's "rationalistic" mode, is especially
important because it may be the typical communication strategy
employed in highly differentiated social systems. Chapter 1 encountered this phenomenon in distinguishing between most primitive
initiation ceremonies and those employed by modern religious or fra
ternal groups. Still another previously cited example is the generalized
character of male solidarity in the Moslem town of Silwa, Egypt.

A review of these other communication strategies inevitably leads
to speculation about their relationship to different types of social struc
ture. It may be that other modes of organization are closely associated
with a particular kind of symbol management in the same way that
solidarity appears to be related to dramatization. An even wider intel
lectual path opens when, with Kenneth Burke,[2] one considers the pos
sibility that the variables of communication are the fundamental inde
pendent variables of sociology and that attempts to "go beyond" avail
able symbols to some basic social reality are in error.

Extensions of the Dramaturgical Framework

The ceremonies that have been considered here may all be classified
as rites of "enhancement." The most straightforward interpretation of
the three scales of status dramatization is that they index the rein
forcement of the initiate's social position within the incorporating
structures. But Harold Garfinkel has called our attention to a type of

[2] An excellent exposition of Burke's position on this and other points is to be
found in Duncan (1962).

ritual which, in contrast, is clearly negative. These "status degradation ceremonies" are directed to "transforming an individual's total identity into an identity lower in the group's scheme of social types" (1956:420). Such ceremonies take many concrete forms: ostracism and exile in Greek and Roman times, cashiering and drumming out, certain practices in Marine training camps, the terminal master's degree, some Congressional inquiries, and, of course, formal criminal proceedings. Although such ceremonies seem to be rare in primitive society—perhaps because rapid death of the degraded so often curtails the social elaboration of ceremony—certain components of ordinary initiation ceremonies might be interpreted as temporary degradation mechanisms. Thus, the treatment of African initiates in the bush camps often surpasses the performance of the most imaginative sergeant in officers' candidate school, and the requirement that girls cover their faces and bodies during menstrual seclusion and accept the interpretation of their state as "unclean" may qualify. Indeed, the menstrual taboos that often apply to native women throughout their middle years may function as a mechanism for reducing the status of women in contrast to that of men.

Despite the rarity of discrete degradation ceremonies in nonliterate communities, it is of interest to question whether they require any substantial reformulation of the solidarity hypothesis. They evidently do not. Garfinkel proposes that "only in societies that are completely demoralized, will an observer be unable to find such ceremonies, since only in total anomie are the conditions of degradation ceremonies lacking" (1956:420). It is a reasonable extension of this to say that the elaboration of the abasement proceedings varies directly with the degree of solidarity. In sociology it is a commonplace that scapegoating is associated with authoritarian structures, of which some at least may correspond to what has here been defined as solidarity. What are unexplained, of course, are the conditions under which a group employs each type.

Almost by definition, ceremonies of enhancement are admission mechanisms, while degradation ceremonies exclude. At least one condition, then, of the occurrence of status reduction is the existence of some segment of society of lower status. It follows that degradation ceremonies should be characteristic of differentiated societies because these more often contain total institutions or degrading enclaves to which an outcast may be sent. Perhaps the mythic elaboration of the "journey to the land of the dead," echoed even in the *Aeneid*, is more characteristic of less complex societies, where about the only alternative to membership in one's own community is participation in the world of the dead.

It is easy to see that the function of degradation ceremonies in solidary groups is essentially the same as that of enhancement ceremonies. Just as initiation dramatizes what the group is, so elaborate exclusion rites communicate what the group is not. The definition of the situation is maintained in both ways. On another theoretical point, however, the interpretation of degradation ceremonies poses difficulties. Garfinkel points out that the "transformation of identities is the destruction of one social object and the constitution of another" (1956:421). Despite the ceremonial elaboration of the destructive side of degradation rites, we can appreciate the possibility that the ritual may also work toward establishing a new identity. If this is so, the interpretation of initiation ceremonies as a simple unidimensional process of enhancement may be inadequate. The very same rituals, or other activity not included in the scale, may deal with the other phase of what is fundamentally a double process. In essence, this is the hypothesis of Van Gennep and Whiting that was rejected in the Introduction, but the possibility that better measures may reveal a twofold process should not be overlooked.

It is unnecessary to dwell on the application of the solidarity hypothesis to other statuses. Van Gennep's great phrase, "rites of passage," brings these possibilities into full prominence. More important is a reconsideration of the distinction between the ceremonies that appear to focus on status transitions and those "rites of intensification" that more obviously pertain to the whole group. A number of facts throw doubt on the conceptual utility of the classification. In the first place, many rites of passage do in fact involve the whole community. Chapter 1 presented evidence on the high frequency of community-wide participation in the boys' ceremonies, and this analysis did not take into account the fact that even when the women or some families are excluded, the whole community usually knows of the event. This is particularly so when the ceremony is delayed until a group of candidates can be assembled. The community-wide nature of status ceremonies is undeniable when the initiate is an important person; in such cases, it is a clear error to restrict their interpretation to a status transition process. A third fact is the frequent combination of status ceremonies with a community seasonal observance.

But more fundamental is the lack of theoretical difference between the two types of ceremony. Both have the same function of dramatizing, and thereby clarifying, the meaning structures maintained by the group. Whether the triggering event is the induction of new recruits or a shift in the dominant subsistence activity consequent to a change of season is immaterial. While it may be useful to speak of limited and general dramatizations, the distinction between community transition and role transition introduces an unnecessary complication.

The nature of cross-cultural data pretty well requires that a study be confined to institutionalized forms of dramatization. But there is no apparent theoretical reason why the solidarity hypothesis should not apply to informal modes of dramatization such as stereotyping, avoidance and deference behavior, and the myriad other little rituals of everyday life. Orrin Klapp (1962) has vividly sketched out a whole new world of verbal dramatizations that take the form of social types. Quisling, egghead, muscle-man, Simon Legree, snake-in-the-grass, and yes-man are only a few of the striking linguistic characterizations available for calling attention to what is hypothesized to be a person's dominant motivation. While every language has a flexible vocabulary of motives that may be pieced together for a more careful statement of a person's apparent behavorial regularities, social types encapsulate in somewhat more stable form the person's presumed total identity. Taken together they constitute a store of prepackaged strategies for social placement. In principle they are not different from the more elaborate initiation ceremony, and indeed, the public labeling of a person as a particular social type may often serve as an informal initiation or degradation ceremony.

The difficulty in applying the solidarity hypothesis to such informal dramatizations is in locating the relevant social structure. Terms like "hatchetman," "apple-polisher," and "rate-buster" have overtones of occupational contexts, but they have been extended and now exist as free-floating symbols available for any situation that requires such symbolic delineation of its component positions. Similarly, the gradations of deference gestures are "stored" in most cultures, readily available for use in situations that have suddenly crystallized organizationally. The solidarity hypothesis leads one to look for the containing structure that must exist rather than for "high-status roles" or "basic values," which more often than not introduce tautologies.

The Individual and the Group

In a recent summary of social psychology, Lambert and Lambert (1964:106ff.) have summarized three answers to what they aptly call the "large question" of the relation between sociocultural and social-psychological processes. The essential notion of the first answer is that social-psychological processes are dependent on the occurrence of the larger sociocultural processes and have no independent causal effect. Thus there are two sets of phenomena, but the former are always determined by the latter events so that there is no great importance to special study of psychological processes. The second answer assumes that the stuff of the one is the stuff of the other, that talking about processes like "diplomacy" and "politics" is simply a shorthand way of referring to the more complex interactions of social-psychological processes, and therefore that the two languages are essentially interchangeable. The third answer asserts that "social-psychological processes are causally important as events that *mediate* or *integrate* the broadly shared events and processes occurring in society and culture, regardless of whether or not society and culture are made of social-psychological stuff" (Lambert and Lambert 1964:107). The last position is, of course, that of Whiting and his associates, and is also represented by the earlier work of Kardiner and Linton (Kardiner 1939). While recognizing the initial determination of structural factors, this psychogenic explanation places more emphasis on individual-level processes than do the first two answers, both of which reject the crucial element of independent causal efficacy for such factors.

Having these three answers at hand provides a needed perspective on the sociogenic-psychogenic dialogue that has pervaded this research, but in the interests of promoting the dialogue and exposing the present study to critical scrutiny, the essential points of contrast must be specified even further. The diagram of causal sequences set forth in Figure 1 (p. 58) has already indicated some points of difference, but because the issue is wider than the two interpretations of initiation ceremonies, it will be useful to illustrate the psychogenic position by another line of research that introduces different variables while retaining the basic paradigm. The work of McClelland, particularly as elaborated in *The Achieving Society* (1961), is the obvious choice. He proposes that a variable of personality, "achievement motivation," is a significant determinant of economic development. Achievement motivation is determined by the type of child-training practices used by families, and these in turn are conditioned by general economic and social factors operating in the wider society. A simplified diagram is shown in Figure 2 (page 160).

Figure 2 organizes the factors according to individual and group levels, as indicated by the solid line. The labels "background factors," "psychological variables," etc., are McClelland's, but they do not obscure the major elements of the paradigm: the channeling of the effects of sociocultural factors through the family, and the inculcation or arousal of a personality factor that "mediates" between the antecedent conditions and the later effects at the sociocultural level. An important point, not shown in the diagram, is that achievement motivation is thought to have an independent effect. If such motivation were simply an inseparable component of the antecedent conditions, there would be less justification for interest. But McClelland's claim is that it is a condition necessary to a rapid rate of economic development and that its effect can be independently analyzed.

It is clear that McClelland's version of the model mutes the combination of Marx and Freud that is so prominent in the Kardiner-Whiting model. His "background factors" are not restricted to economic factors, and the dependent variable is not confined to ideological or "projective" dimensions. However, the essential feature—that sociocultural factors are transmuted into psychological factors, and these into consequent sociocultural effects—is still strong. And what could be more reasonable? Must we not all admit that we as individuals are influenced by the social environment in which we grew up, and that we developed thoughts, feelings, and tendencies that have an effect on the form that our social environment will assume later on? Who can deny that this scheme, which just happens to provide a happy division of labor for sociologists, anthropologists, and psychologists and which appears to duplicate the democratic process of voting, is not at the same time nature's own plan?

On the other hand, the sociogenic position that has been taken in

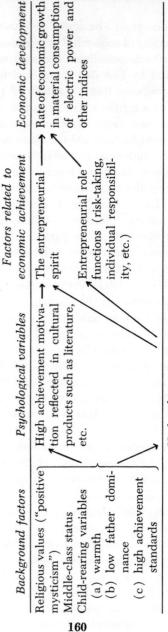

FIGURE 2. Simplified Chart of Interrelationships Among Key Variables Related to Economic Achievement (based on McClelland's diagram [1961:438])

	Factors related to	
Background factors	Psychological variables	economic achievement	Economic development
Religious values ("positive mysticism") Middle-class status Child-rearing variables (a) warmth (b) low father dominance (c) high achievement standards	High achievement motivation reflected in cultural products such as literature, etc. High achievement motivation in individuals	The entrepreneurial spirit Entrepreneurial role functions (risk-taking, individual responsibility, etc.)	Rate of economic growth in material consumption of electric power and other indices

this study is something of a blend of the first two positions outlined by Lambert and Lambert. It assumes that social structure—communities, families, age-sex arrangements, and all the other stable or transient teams and combinations—is made of the same "stuff" as social-psychological processes. But the combination of beliefs, behavioral regularities, etc., that we call personality is one level of organization while social structure is another. Thus, there is an essential difference: the pattern of interlocking loyalties that constitute a thing like male solidarity is not the same as the individual expression of such loyalty. Therefore it is unwise to use the same vocabulary for describing both phenomena; not only are there differences in level of organization, but the vocabulary for one or the other level may not be correct even for its own level. Terms like "politics" and "attitude" are so close to ordinary, unanalyzed speech that they are likely to fade away as work becomes more precise. And even precise vocabularies will come and go according to their merit. This is not to deny the possibility that a frame of reference and its related scientific vocabulary will someday be constructed that will encompass both levels of organization, but that is something different from the essentially reductionist position of the second answer.

If social structure is the *organization* of individual behavior, then there is very little in behavior that is not a part of social structure, although, of course, there is much that is not institutionalized structure. To state that no man is an island is not to make a new claim, but with the widespread use of questionnaires (which only appear to yield individual responses) and the impressive growth of psychological theory, it has been forgotten that all the social sciences should take groups and their interrelations as their object of study. Even the apparent exception of role theory may be construed as the analysis of differentiation and intersections of groups.

In these terms, it makes no sense to talk of an achievement motive as the phrase is currently used. Such a label is misleading if the reality is an interlocking of behavior such that each individual's contribution to the group's "achievement rhetoric" is conditioned by his position in the structure. Very probably it is the group-created and -maintained rhetoric that is tapped when McClelland subjects children's stories and similar public communication to content analysis. And very likely it is a structural aspect that is indexed even when the Thematic Apperception Test is used to elicit what appear to be individual responses: given the stimulus situation in the picture cards, people use the vocabulary of motives that they have picked up in interaction with others. Indeed, using such a pattern of symbols *is* interaction, and just such regularities allow outsiders to know that a social structure exists. Thus, the individual tendencies that are crucial to the mediation model evaporate when viewed in another framework, and the empirical results generated by the model are opened to alternate interpretations.

To say, however, that the sociogenic position allows no place for social-psychological processes is an oversimplification. They are embedded in structural processes. It is true that as the variables are usually formulated, they are granted no independent causal role. If the sociogenic position is correct, analysis will show either that most of the associations between variables like achievement motivation and economic development are spurious, and came about by using faulty concepts and measures, or, alternatively, that they are essentially tautological. Such tautologies take a number of forms. It may be, for instance, that the presence of the achievement rhetoric is simply one aspect of solidarity structures and that the developmental sequence consists of logical inclusion. In another type, a smaller or subordinate structure, such as a family or peer group, functions in a way that is congruent with the effect of the organization of an incorporating structure, such as the community. In this situation, the substructure cannot be ignored even though its effect may not show up as an independent factor. A community with families is quite different from a community without them, and the two may be expected to function differently. Such acknowledgment is not a recognition of causal efficacy, however.

It is at this point that the sociogenic interpretation recognizes the possible independent effect of certain kinds of personality structures—let us call them very small groups containing only one member. Just as under certain conditions a family or community may get into a relationship with a larger incorporating structure in such a way that the outcome is a change in the larger structure, so it may be possible for certain kinds of individuals to have a relationship with a group such that a new equilibrium results. Only extensive empirical investigation will tell us how frequently individuals act as catalysts, but it is doubtful whether these individuals are frequent or strong enough to bring about such changes as economic development.

The difference in the positions is illustrated by an interesting example that McClelland gives (1961:404). He admits that the rapid economic development of Germany between 1925 and 1950 is troublesome for his theory in that the inculcation of achievement motivation at the crucial ages of five through ten or so is usually slower than was the German rate of growth. He does not takes the easy way out and resort to the achievement motivation that might have been left over from previous eras. Instead, he suggests that the absence of so many fathers during the two wars might have provided just the right family structure for producing widespread achievement in the new generation. But why is it necessary to bring in the family at all? Is it not more plausible to hold that the sharp decline in national power after each war, combined after 1945 with the ubiquitous Soviet threat, galvanized the entire nation, young and old, regardless of family structure, to the fervent coordination that produces economic development? Very likely McClelland would not deny this structural effect. In other parts of the book he stresses "ideological fervor" as a crucial precondition of growth. But it never stands alone, capable of changing men directly; it is always transmuted within the family into achievement motivation, inculcated in the child by a kind of "trickle down" process, after which social change really moves ahead.

From this perspective the shortcomings of the psychogenic position are apparent. The paradigm does not explain the thing we really want to know, which is why some groups are organized in one way and others in another. Economic development, for instance, involves above all a different organization of national resources from the unproductive traditional form. While it is interesting to learn that a developed nation may have a high proportion of people who use the achievement rhetoric even in their off moments, that fact does not explain how these people came to be coordinated in a nontraditional way or how they energize the structures within which they work. Moreover, in the emphasis the mediation model gives to childhood socialization, we are being led astray. Very likely the fact that families stress independence training in developed countries is simply another index of the over-all modern social structure, along with the prevalence of the achievement rhetoric. To look for causal relations between two indices of the same phenomena can only lead to confusion.

Thus, the basic claim of this book is that there exists another frame of reference for the analysis of personality and culture, which, while radical in its rejection of the individual as a unit of analysis relevant to the explanation of structure, is at the same time closer to common observation in its emphasis on the multiple teams and institutionalized structures that channel and coordinate individual contributions to the social process. In this area of intergroup relations, the complexities of which social scientists are only now beginning to disentangle, lies our hope of finding true causal relationships. In particular combinations of groups, involving predictable forms of social rhetoric, we ought to find the invariant antecedents of such social forms as solidarity and dramatization.

Appendixes

A. Study Code

Where no code is given, 0 and 1 for "absent" and "present" are to be understood. X stands for doubtful. Use "–" for no data or not applicable.

COLUMN

1–4 Estimated population of the local group under consideration: code actual estimate up to 9,999.

5 Coder's estimate of population trend.
1 Declining
2 Expanding
3 Stable

6 Code highest step on articulation scale.
1 Two or more bisexual social or ceremonial gatherings of the local group per year.
2 Area within the settlement pattern that is considered public—plaza, dance area, area around a public building, etc.
3 Structure that is used exclusively for nondomestic purposes—a temple or clubhouse, etc.
4 Crimes against persons or property punished by group action. Accused is formally charged, and there is a standard procedure of control. An effective colonial authority qualifies.
5 Symbolic medium of exchange—real money—in contrast to barter and exchange as the sole economic mechanism.
6 Full-time bureaucrats unrelated to government head (in contrast to part-time bureaucrats related to government head, or lack of any).
7 Full-time specialized real priest (not diviner or healer), including missionaries if they are at least partially accepted by community.

165

8 Written language used by at least one local person besides the priest.

9 Formal education of both sexes with fulltime specialized teacher.

0 Local group has same culture as dominant society (in contrast to partially assimilated groups, ethnic subcultures, etc.).

7 Scale error in articulation scale: code number of scale step in which error occurs.

8 Lack of data for a given scale step: code number of step.

9 Subsistence type. A typology based on Murdock's column 1. (Murdock 1957).

  1 Modern agriculture: cultivation of cereal grains and integration of large domesticated animals that have been introduced through European contact.

  2 Traditional agriculture: cultivation of cereal grains where large domestic animals are either aboriginal or unimportant.

  3 Horticulture: cultivation of roots, tubers, tree fruits, or starches. Role of domesticated animals ignored.

  4 Gathering: no cultivation. Subsistence based on gathering, hunting, fishing, or combinations of these.

10 Family types. Murdock's column 7.

  1 Extended families

  2 Independent families

  3 Lineal families

  4 Stem families

11 Primary marital residence. Murdock's column 8.

  0 Avunculocal

  1 Bilocal

  2 Duolocal

  3 Matrilocal

  4 Neolocal

  5 Patrilocal

  6 Duopatrilocal

  7 Sororilocal

  8 Uxoripatrilocal

  9 Others (uxoriavunculocal, uxorineolocal, uxoribilocal, viravunculocal, duoavunculocal)

12 Proportion of households in which husband has more than one wife. Murdock's column 9.

    1   Monogamy customary in all households

    2   Limited polygyny, less than 20 per cent of households and typically confined to wealthy or powerful men

    3   General, 20 per cent or more

13 Multifemale household organization. A typology based on family type and extent of polygyny.

    1   Independent families with monogamous unions only

    2   Stem or lineal families, and/or limited polygyny

    3   Extended families, and/or general polygyny

14 Village-wide, exclusively female groups or organized activity other than work groups.

15 Village-wide, exclusively female work groups.

16 Cooperative female domestic work groups either among women of a large household or among neighboring households, but excluding casual neighboring.

17 Code highest step on male solidarity scale.

    0   Informal solidarity that does not attain the generality or behavioral expression specified in step 1.

    1   Exclusive male activity participated in by all adult males and protected by physical or normative perception barriers.

    2   Ritualization of male activity, at least in part.

    3   Definite ranking of men within the activity.

    4   Training or planning for war a part of activity.

18 Scale error in male solidarity scale.

19 Lack of data for steps in male solidarity scale.

20 Village-wide, exclusively male work groups.

    0   None

    1   Hunting

    2   Fishing

    3   Herding

21 Intercommunity armed conflict.

    0   Absent, or personal fights only.

    1   Supralocal conflict: communities supply men for larger army and community identity tends to be merged.

2   Present local warfare: conflict involving groups of men representing their community took place within adult lives of living men.

3   Past local warfare: intercommunity conflict took place before adulthood of community men.

22 Code highest step on male sex-role dramatization scale.
    0   Undramatic recognition only (following items not present).
    1   Customary minimal social recognition (gift, party, change of name, etc.).
    2   Personal dramatization (initiate is ceremonially dressed or adorned).
    3   Organized social response (group dresses up and/or performs).
    4   Affective social response (beating or severe hazing of initiates).

23 Scale error in male dramatization scale.

24 Lack of data in male dramatization scale.

25 Code highest step of female sex-role dramatization scale. Items are the same as male scale given in column 22 above.

26 Scale error in female dramatization scale.

27 Lack of data in female dramatization scale.

28 Customary separation of male adolescents' sleeping quarters.

29 Male initiates socially or physically secluded.

30 Male initiates give public performance.

31 Male initiates restricted by taboos or ritual requirements.

32 Male initiates the object of emotionalized group responses other than beating or hazing.

33 Paid specialist participates in the ceremony for males.

34 Large feast to which all in local group are invited.

35 Genital operations performed.

36 Evidence of decline or attenuation of male ceremony.

37 Number of days required for ceremony.

    1   Up to a week
    2   Week or more

38 Number of male initiates usually involved in ceremony.
   1 Usually one, but occasionally two candidates.
   2 Two or more.

39 Relationship of male initiation ceremony to formal organizations.
   0 Not part of the context of a community organization
   1 Part of the context of such an organization

40 Size of audience during the public phase of male initiation ceremony.
   1 Family or close friends only
   2 Part or all of community

41 Customary separation of female adolescents' sleeping quarters.

42 Female initiates socially or physically secluded.

43 Female initiates give public performance.

44 Female initiates restricted by taboos or ritual requirements.

45 Female initiates the object of emotionalized group response other than beating or hazing.

46 Paid specialist participates in ceremony for females.

47 Large feast to which all in local group are invited.

48 Genital operations performed.

49 Evidence of decline or attentuation of female ceremony.

50 Number of days required for ceremony.
   1 Up to a week
   2 Week or more

51 Number of female initiates usually involved in ceremony.
   1 Usually one, but occasionally two candidates
   2 Two or more

52 Relationship of female initiation ceremony to formal organizations.
   0 Not part of the context of a community organization
   1 Part of the context of such an organization

53 Size of audience during public phase of female initiation.
   1 Family or close friends only
   2 Part or all of community

54 Code highest step in scale of dramatization of parenthood.

0 No community-wide ritual requirements or prohibitions on parents before or after birth or directed toward newborn, or are informal only.

1 Special attention to or concern for welfare of newborn other than normal cleansing.

2 Ritual restrictions or requirements on mother during pregnancy period.

3 Ritual restrictions or requirements on father during pregnancy period.

4 Ritual restrictions or requirements on father after birth of child.

5 Seclusion of mother at time of birth or immediately thereafter.

55 Scale error in parenthood dramatization scale.

56 Lack of data for a given scale step: code step number.

57 Exclusive mother-son sleeping arrangement.

58 Boyhood ceremony.

59 Male childhood ceremony.

60 Girlhood ceremony.

61 Female childhood ceremony.

62 Family maintains a barrier to intrusion other than domestic quarters per se, i.e., a wall, fence, brush barrier, or intentional seclusion from outsider, and/or there is a symbolic focus such as a shrine, house crest, guest house, etc.

63 Typology of female solidarity (combining columns 16 and 62).
  1 No female work group or boundary
  2 Female work groups only
  3 Boundary only
  4 Female work groups and boundary

64 Clan organization (as coded by Murdock in the Ethnographic atlas. 1962:113 ff.), Column 6.
  1 Agamous communities without localized clans or any marked tendency toward either local exogamy or local endogamy.
  2 Clan communities, each consisting essentially of a single localized kin group or clan.
  3 Demes, i.e., communities revealing a marked tendency toward local endogamy but not segmented into clan barrios.
  4 Exogamous communities, i.e., those revealing a marked ten-

dency toward local exogamy without having the specific structure of clans.

5 Segmented communities, i.e., those divided into barrios, wards, or hamlets, each of which is essentially a localized kin group or clan, in the absence of any indication of local exogamy. Large extended families . . . are here treated as clan barrios if they are integrated by a rule of ambilineal, matrilineal, or patrilineal descent, but are ignored if descent is bilateral.

6 Segmented communities where a marked tendency toward local exogamy is also specifically reported.

65 Post-partum taboo on women's sex relations.
  0 None
  1 Short (less than a year)
  2 Long (year or more)

66–67 Serial number

B. Classification of Study Sample Societies

SOCIETY	1	2	3	4	5	6	7	8	9	10	11	12
Alorese	0	1	8	0	3	6	3	–	2	2	5	2
Araucanians	0	1	1	1	2	9	–	8	2	3	5	2
Ashanti	X	X	X	X	2	7	–	5	3	3	9	3
Azande	0	0	5	0	X	6	–	2	2	2	5	3
Balinese	0	3	0	0	2	9	–	–	2	1	5	2
Bontoc Igorot	2	0	0	0	2	5	–	–	2	2	5	1
Cagaba	0	2	5	0	3	7	–	–	3	2	3	3
Camayura	0	1	1	0	1	4	–	–	3	1	8	2
Chagga	X	X	X	X	X	4	–	–	2	2	5	3
Cheyenne	0	0	5	0	1	4	–	–	4	1	3	3
Chiricahua	0	0	5	0	3	3	–	–	4	1	3	2
Dahomeans	1	0	0	0	X	7	–	–	3	1	5	3
Egyptians	3	5	0	0	2	0	–	–	2	3	8	2
Eskimos	0	0	2	5	1	2	0	0	4	2	1	2
Fijians	0	1	2	5	2	9	–	–	3	2	5	1
French	2	0	0	0	2	0	–	–	1	2	4	1
Ganda	X	X	X	X	1	7	–	–	3	2	5	3
Hopi	0	2	5	0	3	9	7	–	2	1	3	1
Japanese	1	6	6	3	1	0	–	–	1	4	5	1
Jivaro	0	0	2	5	1	1	–	–	3	1	8	3
Koryak	0	1	0	0	1	6	–	–	4	3	8	2
Kwakiutl	0	5	0	0	1	2	–	–	4	1	5	1
Kwoma	0	1	0	0	X	5	–	–	3	2	5	3
Lakhers	0	3	5	0	3	6	3	–	2	2	5	1
Lamba	0	1	4	4	X	7	–	–	2	2	9	2
Lapps	0	1	0	0	1	9	6	–	2	2	8	1
Lepchas	0	1	7	6	1	8	–	–	2	3	5	2
Malaita	0	0	3	5	1	5	–	–	3	2	5	2
Maori	0	2	1	0	1	3	–	–	3	1	1	2
Mexicans	3	5	0	0	2	0	–	–	1	2	5	1
Mixtec	0	6	0	0	2	9	–	–	1	1	5	1
Navaho	0	5	0	0	2	9	–	–	1	1	3	2
New Ireland	0	2	3	2	X	8	–	–	3	2	3	2
Nuer	0	0	7	5	2	3	–	–	2	3	8	3
Nyakyusa	0	2	0	0	2	9	8	–	3	2	4	3
Ojibwa	0	0	4	5	2	3	–	–	4	2	8	2
Ontong Javanese	0	1	0	0	1	5	–	–	3	1	3	2
Ooldea	0	2	0	0	3	9	–	2	4	2	5	3
Papago	0	2	5	0	2	9	–	–	1	3	5	1
Pilaga	0	1	2	7	X	2	1	–	4	2	8	2
Pondo	X	X	X	X	2	9	–	–	2	3	5	3
Samoans	X	X	X	X	X	7	5	–	3	1	1	2
Serbs	2	1	8	2	2	0	–	–	1	3	5	1
Siriono	0	0	7	5	1	1	–	–	2	1	3	3
Tallensi	X	X	X	X	2	6	–	–	2	3	5	3
Tanala	0	3	7	5	3	8	–	–	2	1	5	3
Thonga	0	0	5	0	2	6	–	–	2	1	5	3
Timbira	0	2	2	6	3	4	–	5	4	3	3	1
Tiv	0	5	0	0	X	9	–	–	3	1	5	3
Trobrianders	0	3	0	0	1	2	–	–	3	2	0	2
Trukese	0	2	3	0	2	9	–	–	3	2	3	2
U.S.	0	2	3	2	1	0	–	–	1	2	4	1
Yagua	0	0	3	5	1	1	–	–	3	2	8	1
Yap	0	0	3	7	1	9	–	–	3	1	5	1

13	14	15	16	17	18	19	20	21	22	23	24	25	26	27	28	29	30
2	0	0	0	0	–	–	1	3	0	–	–	1	–	–	0	–	–
2	0	0	0	0	–	–	0	3	0	–	–	0	–	–	0	–	–
3	0	0	1	0	–	–	0	1	0	–	–	3	–	–	0	–	–
3	0	0	0	0	–	–	1	1	3	–	–	0	–	–	1	1	1
3	0	0	0	3	–	–	3	1	2	–	–	3	–	–	0	1	0
1	0	1	0	4	–	–	3	2	0	–	–	0	–	–	1	–	–
3	0	0	0	3	–	–	0	0	2	–	–	2	1	–	1	1	0
3	0	0	1	2	–	–	2	2	2	–	–	2	–	–	0	1	0
3	0	0	0	3	2	–	3	3	2	–	3	3	–	–	1	1	1
3	1	0	1	4	–	–	1	2	1	–	–	2	–	–	0	0	1
3	0	0	1	0	–	–	1	2	0	–	–	3	–	–	1	–	–
3	0	0	1	3	–	1	3	1	3	–	–	4	–	–	1	0	0
2	0	0	1	3	–	–	3	1	0	–	–	1	–	–	1	–	–
2	0	1	1	0	–	–	0	0	0	–	–	0	–	–	0	–	–
1	0	1	0	1	–	–	1	3	2	–	–	0	–	–	1	1	0
1	0	0	0	0	–	–	0	1	0	–	–	0	–	–	0	–	–
3	0	0	1	0	–	–	1	1	0	–	–	1	–	–	1	–	–
3	1	0	0	3	–	–	1	3	4	–	2	2	–	–	1	1	1
2	0	0	0	0	–	–	0	1	0	–	–	0	–	–	0	–	–
3	0	1	1	0	–	–	1	2	2	–	–	2	–	–	1	1	0
2	0	0	1	0	–	–	0	1	0	–	–	0	–	–	0	–	–
3	0	0	0	3	–	–	0	2	3	–	–	1	–	–	0	1	1
3	0	1	1	4	–	–	1	2	4	–	–	2	–	3	0	1	1
1	0	0	1	0	–	–	3	3	0	–	–	0	–	–	1	–	–
2	0	1	1	0	–	–	0	3	0	–	–	4	–	–	1	–	–
1	0	0	0	0	–	–	3	0	0	0	–	0	0	–	0	–	–
2	0	0	1	0	–	–	3	0	0	–	–	0	–	–	0	–	–
2	0	0	0	0	–	–	0	2	0	–	–	0	–	–	1	–	–
3	0	0	0	0	–	–	0	2	0	–	–	0	–	–	0	–	–
1	0	0	0	0	–	–	0	1	0	–	–	1	–	–	0	–	–
3	0	0	–	0	–	–	0	1	0	–	–	0	–	–	0	–	–
3	0	0	0	2	–	–	3	1	0	–	–	2	–	–	1	–	–
2	0	1	1	2	–	–	1	3	3	–	–	3	–	–	1	1	1
3	0	0	1	3	–	–	1	2	3	–	–	0	–	–	1	1	0
3	0	0	1	0	–	–	1	3	0	–	–	3	–	–	1	–	–
2	0	0	1	0	–	–	1	2	2	–	–	2	–	–	0	1	0
3	0	0	0	2	–	3	0	3	1	–	–	2	–	–	0	0	0
3	0	0	0	3	–	–	0	0	4	–	–	1	–	–	1	1	0
2	0	0	1	0	–	–	3	1	0	–	–	1	–	–	1	–	–
2	0	0	0	0	–	–	0	1	0	–	–	0	–	–	0	–	–
3	0	0	1	0	–	–	3	1	0	–	–	3	–	–	0	–	–
3	1	1	0	2	–	–	0	3	1	–	–	1	–	–	0	0	0
2	0	0	1	0	–	–	0	1	0	–	–	0	–	–	0	–	–
3	0	0	1	0	–	–	0	0	0	–	–	3	–	–	0	–	–
3	0	0	0	0	–	–	1	3	0	–	–	0	–	–	1	–	–
3	0	0	1	0	–	–	3	3	0	–	–	0	–	–	1	–	–
3	0	1	0	4	2	–	3	1	4	–	–	3	2	–	1	1	1
2	0	0	0	3	–	–	1	2	4	–	–	0	–	–	1	1	1
3	0	0	1	1	–	–	0	3	2	–	–	1	–	–	1	1	0
2	0	0	0	0	–	–	0	3	0	–	–	0	–	–	1	–	–
2	0	0	1	0	–	–	0	3	0	–	–	0	–	–	1	–	–
1	0	0	0	0	–	–	0	1	0	–	–	0	–	–	0	–	–
1	0	1	0	0	–	–	1	0	0	–	–	1	–	–	0	–	–
3	1	0	0	4	–	–	2	3	1	–	–	1	–	–	1	0	–

SOCIETY	31	32	33	34	35	36	37	38	39	40	41	42	43	44	45	46
Alorese	–	–	–	–	–	–	–	–	–	–	0	–	–	–	–	–
Araucanians	–	–	–	–	–	1	–	–	–	–	0	–	–	–	–	–
Ashanti	–	–	–	–	–	–	–	–	–	–	0	0	0	1	0	X
Azande	1	0	1	0	1	0	2	2	0	1	0	–	–	–	–	–
Balinese	1	0	1	1	0	1	1	1	0	2	0	1	1	1	0	0
Bontoc Igorot	–	–	–	–	0	X	–	–	–	–	0	–	–	–	–	–
Cagaba	1	1	0	0	0	0	1	1	0	1	0	1	0	1	1	0
Camayura	1	0	0	0	0	0	2	1	0	1	0	1	0	1	0	0
Chagga	1	1	0	0	1	1	1	2	0	1	0	1	1	0	1	0
Cheyenne	0	0	0	0	0	0	1	1	0	1	0	1	0	1	0	0
Chiricahua	–	–	–	–	–	–	–	–	–	–	0	1	1	1	0	0
Dahomeans	1	1	1	0	1	1	1	2	0	2	0	1	0	1	1	0
Egyptians	–	–	–	–	–	–	–	–	–	–	0	1	0	1	1	1
Eskimos	–	–	–	–	–	–	–	–	–	–	0	–	–	–	–	–
Fijians	1	0	1	1	1	0	2	2	0	2	0	–	–	–	–	–
French	–	–	–	–	–	–	–	–	–	–	0	–	–	–	–	–
Ganda	–	–	–	–	–	–	–	–	–	–	1	1	1	0	–	–
Hopi	1	1	0	X	0	1	2	2	1	2	0	1	1	1	0	–
Japanese	–	–	–	–	–	–	–	–	–	–	0	–	–	–	–	–
Jivaro	1	1	0	1	0	–	1	1	0	2	1	1	0	1	0	0
Koryak	–	–	–	–	–	–	–	–	–	–	0	–	–	–	–	–
Kwakiutl	1	1	0	1	0	1	2	2	1	2	0	1	0	1	0	0
Kwoma	1	1	0	1	1	0	2	2	0	2	0	1	1	1	X	X
Lakhers	–	–	–	–	–	–	–	–	–	–	0	–	–	–	–	–
Lamba	–	–	–	–	–	–	–	–	–	–	0	1	1	1	1	1
Lapps	–	–	–	–	–	–	–	–	–	–	0	–	–	–	–	–
Lepchas	–	–	–	–	–	–	–	–	–	–	0	–	–	–	–	–
Malaita	–	–	–	–	–	–	–	–	–	–	0	–	–	–	–	–
Maori	–	–	–	–	–	–	–	–	–	–	0	–	–	–	–	–
Mexicans	–	–	–	–	–	–	–	–	–	–	0	0	0	–	–	–
Mixtec	–	–	–	–	–	–	–	–	–	–	0	–	–	–	–	–
Navaho	–	–	–	–	–	–	–	–	–	–	0	1	0	1	0	1
New Ireland	0	1	0	1	1	0	2	2	0	2	0	0	0	0	0	1
Nuer	1	1	0	1	0	0	2	2	0	1	0	–	–	–	–	–
Nyakyusa	–	–	–	–	–	–	–	–	–	–	0	1	1	1	0	0
Ojibwa	0	0	0	0	0	0	2	1	0	1	0	1	0	1	0	0
Ontong Java	0	0	0	1	0	0	1	2	0	2	0	0	1	0	0	0
Ooldea	1	1	0	0	1	1	2	2	1	2	1	1	0	0	0	0
Papago	–	–	–	–	–	–	–	–	–	–	1	0	0	1	0	–
Pilaga	–	–	–	–	–	–	–	–	–	–	0	–	–	–	–	–
Pondo	–	–	–	–	–	1	–	–	–	–	0	1	1	1	0	0
Samoans	0	0	0	0	0	1	1	1	1	2	0	0	0	0	0	0
Serbs	–	–	–	–	–	–	–	–	–	–	0	–	–	–	–	–
Siriono	–	–	–	–	–	–	–	–	–	–	0	1	1	1	0	0
Tallensi	–	–	–	–	–	–	–	–	–	–	0	–	–	–	–	–
Tanala	–	–	–	–	–	–	–	–	–	–	0	–	–	–	–	–
Thonga	1	1	0	0	1	0	2	2	0	2	1	1	1	1	1	0
Timbira	1	1	0	1	0	1	2	2	1	2	0	0	0	–	–	–
Tiv	1	0	1	0	1	1	1	2	0	2	0	0	–	–	–	–
Trobrianders	–	–	–	–	–	–	–	–	–	–	1	–	–	–	–	–
Trukese	–	–	–	–	–	–	–	–	–	–	0	–	–	–	–	–
U.S.	–	–	–	–	–	–	–	–	–	–	0	–	–	–	–	–
Yagua	–	–	–	–	–	–	–	–	–	–	0	1	0	1	0	–
Yap	–	0	0	0	0	0	1	1	0	1	0	1	0	1	0	–

48	49	50	51	52	53	54	55	56	57	58	59	60	61	62	63	64	65	66	67
–	–	1	2	0	2	4	–	–	0	1	0	1	0	0	1	4	2	0	1
–	1	–	–	–	–	1	–	–	0	0	0	0	0	0	1	5	0	0	2
0	X	2	1	0	1	3	–	–	–	0	0	0	0	1	4	1	1	0	3
–	–	–	–	–	–	3	–	–	1	0	0	0	0	1	3	1	2	0	4
0	1	1	1	0	1	4	–	–	0	0	1	0	1	1	3	3	0	0	5
–	X	–	–	–	–	0	–	–	0	1	1	0	1	0	1	5	0	0	6
0	0	1	1	0	1	5	–	–	1	1	0	1	0	–	–	1	0	0	7
0	0	2	1	0	1	4	–	–	1	1	0	1	0	1	4	1	0	0	8
1	0	1	2	0	1	5	–	–	1	1	1	1	0	1	3	2	2	0	9
0	0	1	1	0	1	2	–	–	1	1	0	1	0	0	2	4	2	1	0
0	0	1	1	0	2	3	–	–	–	0	1	0	1	1	4	1	2	1	1
0	0	X	2	0	2	2	–	3	1	0	0	0	0	1	4	5	1	1	2
1	0	2	1	0	1	2	–	–	1	1	0	1	0	1	4	3	0	1	3
–	–	–	–	–	–	1	–	–	0	0	0	0	0	0	2	3	0	1	4
–	–	–	–	–	–	4	–	4	1	0	0	0	0	0	1	5	2	1	5
–	–	–	–	–	–	0	–	–	0	0	0	0	0	0	1	1	0	1	6
–	0	1	1	0	1	2	–	–	0	0	0	0	0	0	1	4	4	2	7
–	1	1	2	0	1	1	5	3	0	1	0	1	0	0	1	1	0	1	8
–	–	–	–	–	–	0	–	–	1	0	0	0	0	0	1	1	0	1	9
0	0	1	1	0	1	4	–	–	–	0	1	1	1	1	4	3	2	2	0
–	–	–	–	–	–	1	–	4	–	0	0	0	0	0	2	1	0	2	1
0	1	1	1	0	1	3	–	–	0	0	0	0	0	1	3	4	2	2	2
0	0	X	1	0	X	5	3	–	1	0	0	0	0	0	2	5	2	2	3
–	–	–	–	–	–	4	–	–	0	0	0	0	0	0	2	1	0	2	4
0	0	2	2	0	2	4	3	–	0	1	0	1	0	0	2	1	0	2	5
–	–	–	–	–	–	X	X	–	–	0	1	0	1	0	1	4	X	2	6
–	–	–	–	–	–	5	–	–	0	0	1	0	1	0	2	4	0	2	7
–	–	–	–	–	–	0	–	–	–	0	0	0	0	1	3	1	2	2	8
–	–	–	–	–	–	2	–	–	–	0	1	0	1	1	3	5	0	2	9
–	0	1	1	0	1	2	–	–	0	0	0	0	0	0	1	5	1	3	0
–	–	–	–	–	–	–	–	–	0	X	X	X	X	–	–	5	0	3	1
0	1	1	1	0	2	3	–	–	0	1	0	1	0	1	3	1	0	3	2
0	0	1	1	0	2	3	–	–	1	0	0	0	0	1	4	5	2	3	3
–	–	–	–	–	–	1	–	4	1	1	0	1	0	1	4	2	2	3	4
0	1	2	1	0	2	4	–	4	1	0	0	0	0	1	4	4	2	3	5
0	0	1	1	0	1	2	–	–	0	1	1	1	1	0	2	2	2	3	6
0	0	1	2	0	2	0	–	1	0	0	0	0	0	0	1	1	1	3	7
0	1	1	1	0	1	1	–	–	–	0	0	0	0	0	1	5	2	3	8
–	1	1	1	0	1	3	1	–	0	0	0	0	0	1	4	1	0	3	9
–	–	–	–	–	–	3	–	–	1	0	1	0	1	0	1	–	1	4	0
0	1	2	1	0	2	4	–	–	0	0	0	0	0	1	4	5	2	4	1
0	1	1	1	1	2	3	–	4	1	0	0	0	0	1	3	5	0	4	2
–	–	–	–	–	–	2	–	3	0	0	0	0	0	0	2	5	0	4	3
0	0	1	2	0	1	4	–	–	0	0	0	0	0	0	2	5	0	4	4
–	–	–	–	–	–	5	–	–	0	0	0	0	0	1	3	2	0	4	5
–	–	–	–	–	–	3	–	1	–	1	0	X	0	0	2	5	0	4	6
0	0	2	2	0	2	5	3	–	0	0	0	0	0	1	3	2	1	4	7
–	1	–	–	–	–	5	–	–	–	0	0	0	0	0	1	5	1	4	8
–	–	1	1	0	1	1	–	2	0	1	0	1	0	1	4	2	X	4	9
–	–	–	–	–	–	2	–	–	1	X	X	X	X	0	1	5	2	5	0
–	–	1	–	0	0	3	1	0	0	0	0	0	0	0	2	5	1	5	1
–	–	–	–	–	–	0	–	–	0	0	0	0	0	0	1	1	0	5	2
–	–	2	1	0	1	1	4	–	0	0	0	0	0	0	1	2	1	5	3
–	–	1	1	0	X	3	–	–	0	0	0	0	0	0	1	5	2	5	4

C. Classification of Auxiliary Sample Societies

SOCIETY	1	2	3	4	5	6	7	8	9	10	11	12	13	14	15	16	17
Andamanese	0	0	4	5	1	2	–	–	4	2	1	1	1	0	0	0	0
Aranda	0	0	4	0	1	3	–	–	4	2	5	3	3	1	0	1	4
Azande	0	0	5	0	X	6	–	2	2	2	5	3	3	0	0	0	0
Collinago	0	0	0	1	3	3	–	–	3	1	3	2	3	0	0	1	4
Comanche	0	1	5	0	X	1	–	–	4	1	1	3	3	0	0	1	4
Ila	1	1	5	0	X	9	–	–	2	3	5	3	3	1	1	1	2
Katab	0	1	9	1	X	6	2	1	2	–	–	3	3	0	0	1	2
Lovedu	0	6	1	0	2	8	–	–	2	2	5	3	3	1	0	1	3
Luo	0	0	4	9	X	4	–	–	2	3	5	3	3	0	0	0	0
Malekula	0	0	8	0	1	6	–	6	3	2	5	3	3	1	0	X	4
Mandan	0	3	1	9	1	3	–	–	4	3	3	3	3	1	0	1	3
Marquesans	X	X	X	X	1	3	–	–	3	2	5	1	1	0	0	0	4
Mossi	7	0	0	0	X	9	–	–	2	2	5	3	3	0	0	1	3
New Ireland	0	2	3	2	X	8	–	–	3	2	3	2	2	0	1	1	2
Ojibwa	0	0	4	5	2	3	–	–	4	2	8	2	2	0	0	1	0
Shilluk	X	X	X	X	1	4	–	–	3	2	5	3	3	0	0	0	4
Southeast Salish	X	X	X	X	1	3	–	–	4	–	–	3	3	1	1	1	2
Tapirape	0	1	4	7	1	3	–	–	3	1	3	1	3	0	0	0	4
Tasmanians	0	0	4	9	X	1	–	4	4	2	5	2	2	0	0	0	3
Tikopia	1	2	0	0	2	4	8	–	3	2	5	2	2	1	1	X	2
Timbira	0	2	2	6	3	4	–	5	4	3	3	1	1	0	0	0	3
Tiv	0	5	0	0	X	9	–	–	3	1	5	3	3	0	0	1	1
Wolof	0	1	3	5	2	8	–	–	3	3	5	3	3	0	0	1	2
Yokuts	0	1	0	0	1	5	4	1	4	1	8	2	3	0	0	0	1
Zuni	1	6	6	4	1	9	7	9	2	1	3	1	3	0	0	1	3

SOCIETY	41	42	43	44	45	46	47	48	49	50	51	52
Andamanese	1	1	1	1	0	0	0	0	0	1	1	0
Aranda	0	1	X	1	0	0	0	0	0	1	1	0
Azande	0	–	–	–	–	–	–	–	–	–	–	–
Collinago	0	0	0	1	0	0	1	0	0	2	1	0
Comanche	0	0	0	–	–	–	–	–	–	–	–	–
Ila	1	1	1	1	1	0	1	0	1	2	1	0
Katab	0	0	–	–	–	–	–	–	–	–	–	–
Lovedu	1	1	0	1	1	0	1	0	1	1	1	0
Luo	1	1	0	0	0	0	1	0	0	1	2	0
Malekula	1	X	–	–	–	–	–	–	–	–	–	–
Mandan	0	1	X	1	X	–	–	–	X	1	1	1
Marquesans	0	1	0	1	0	0	0	0	0	1	1	0
Mossi	0	1	0	1	1	0	0	1	0	2	2	1
New Ireland	0	0	0	0	0	1	1	0	0	1	1	0
Ojibwa	0	1	0	1	0	0	0	0	0	1	1	0
Shilluk	1	X	X	X	X	X	X	X	X	X	2	X
Southeast Salish	0	1	0	1	0	0	0	0	0	2	1	0
Tapirape	0	0	0	1	0	–	–	–	–	2	1	0
Tasmanians	0	0	–	–	–	–	–	–	–	–	–	–
Tikopia	0	0	1	0	0	0	1	0	1	X	X	0
Timbira	0	0	–	–	–	–	–	–	1	–	–	–
Tiv	0	0	–	–	–	–	–	–	–	1	1	0
Wolof	0	0	–	–	–	–	–	–	–	1	1	0
Yokuts	0	0	0	1	0	0	–	–	–	1	1	X
Zuni	X	X	X	–	–	–	–	–	–	1	1	0

18	19	20	21	22	23	24	25	26	27	28	29	30	31	32	33	34	35	36	37	38	39	40
–	–	1	2	2	–	–	2	–	–	1	0	1	1	0	0	0	0	1	2	1	0	2
–	4	0	2	3	–	–	3	–	–	1	1	1	1	1	0	0	1	0	2	2	1	2
–	–	1	1	3	–	–	0	–	–	1	1	1	1	0	1	0	1	0	2	2	0	1
2	–	0	2	4	–	–	2	–	–	0	0	1	1	1	0	1	0	0	2	1	0	2
1	–	1	2	3	2	1	0	–	–	1	1	1	1	0	1	1	0	0	1	1	1	1
–	–	3	4	2	–	–	3	–	–	1	1	0	1	0	1	0	1	1	1	2	0	2
–	–	1	4	4	3	1	0	–	–	0	X	0	0	1	0	1	0	1	1	2	1	2
–	–	3	1	4	–	–	4	–	–	1	1	1	1	0	0	0	1	1	2	2	0	2
–	–	3	2	2	–	–	2	–	–	1	1	0	0	0	0	0	0	0	1	2	0	1
–	–	–	2	4	2	–	X	X	X	1	1	1	1	1	0	1	1	0	2	2	0	2
–	–	1	2	3	2	–	1	–	3	0	1	1	1	1	0	1	0	0	1	2	0	2
–	–	2	2	3	–	–	2	–	–	0	0	1	0	1	1	1	1	0	2	2	0	1
–	–	1	4	3	–	–	2	–	–	1	1	1	1	0	1	0	1	1	2	2	1	1
–	–	1	4	3	–	–	3	–	–	1	1	1	0	1	0	1	1	0	2	2	0	2
–	–	1	2	2	–	–	2	–	–	0	1	0	0	0	0	0	0	0	2	1	0	1
–	–	3	2	3	–	4	2	–	1	1	X	1	1	X	X	X	X	1	X	2	1	2
–	–	2	2	2	–	–	2	–	–	0	1	0	0	0	0	0	0	0	1	1	0	1
–	–	1	2	4	3	–	2	1	–	1	1	1	1	0	–	–	–	–	1	1	0	X
–	4	1	2	2	–	3	0	–	–	X	X	1	1	X	–	–	–	–	–	–	0	2
–	–	2	0	3	–	–	2	–	–	0	1	0	1	1	0	1	1	1	1	2	0	2
–	–	1	2	4	–	–	0	–	–	1	1	1	1	1	0	1	0	1	2	2	1	2
–	–	0	4	2	–	–	1	–	–	1	1	0	1	0	1	0	1	1	1	2	0	2
–	–	3	4	4	–	–	1	–	–	0	1	1	1	0	1	0	1	0	1	2	0	2
–	–	0	0	1	–	–	4	3	–	0	1	0	0	0	–	–	–	–	1	1	0	1
–	–	0	4	4	–	–	1	–	2	0	0	1	1	1	0	1	0	0	1	2	1	2

53	54	55	56
1	4	–	–
2	3	–	4
–	3	–	–
X	4	–	3
0	1	3	–
2	2	–	4
0	2	1	–
2	X	X	X
1	X	X	X
X	3	–	–
2	1	–	–
1	3	–	4
1	2	1	–
2	3	–	–
1	2	–	–
X	1	–	4
1	4	–	–
1	4	–	–
–	X	X	X
2	1	–	3
–	4	–	–
1	1	–	2
1	1	–	4
1	4	–	–
1	4	–	–

References

Aberle, D. F., A. K. Cohen, A. K. Davis, M. J. Levy, and F. X. Sutton, 1950. The functional prerequisites of a society. *Ethics, 60,* 100-11.

Aronson, Elliot, and Judson Mills, 1959. The effect of severity of initiation on liking for a group. *Journal of Abnormal and Social Psychology, 59,* 177-81.

Bales, R. F., 1943. The equilibrium problem in small groups. In T. Parsons, R. F. Bales, and E. A. Shils, *Working papers in the theory of action.* Glencoe, Ill.: Free Press.

Benedict, Ruth, 1948. *Patterns of culture.* New York: Mentor Books.

Bettelheim, Bruno, 1954. *Symbolic wounds, puberty rites and the envious male.* Glencoe, Ill.: Free Press.

Burke, Kenneth, 1954. *Permanence and change: an anatomy of purpose,* rev. ed. Los Altos, Calif.: Hermes Publications.

——, 1962. *A grammar of motives and a rhetoric of motives,* in one vol. Cleveland: World Publishing Company.

Burton, Robert V., and J. W. M. Whiting, 1961. The absent father and cross-sex identity. *Merrill-Palmer Quarterly, 7,* 85-95.

Cancian, Francesca, 1960. Functional analysis of change. *American Sociological Review, 25,* 818-27.

Chapple, E. D., and C. S. Coon, 1942. *Principles of anthropology.* New York: Henry Holt and Company.

Charles, Lucille H., 1946. Growing up through drama. *Journal of American Folklore, 59,* 247-67.

Davis, Kingsley, and Judith Blake, 1956. Social structure and fertility: an analytic framework. *Economic Development and Cultural Change, 4,* 231-35.

Driver, Harold E., 1961. Introduction to statistics for comparative research. In Frank W. Moore (ed.), *Readings in cross-cultural methodology.* New Haven: Human Relations Area Files.

Duncan, Hugh D., 1962. *Communication and the social order.* New York: Bedminster Press.

Durkheim, E., 1954. *The elementary forms of the religious life.* Glencoe, Ill.: Free Press.

Eliade, Mircea, 1958. *Birth and rebirth: the religious meanings of initiation in human culture.* Tr. Willard R. Trask. New York: Harper & Brothers.

Ethnographic atlas, 1962. *Ethnology, 1,* 118-23.

Firth, Raymond, 1936. *We, the Tikopia.* New York: American Book Company.

Freeman, L. C., and R. F. Winch, 1957. Societal complexity: an empirical test of a typology of societies. *American Journal of Sociology, 57,* 461-66.

Fried, Morton, 1957. The classification of corporate unilineal descent groups. *Journal of the Royal Anthropological Institute, 87,* 1-29.

Garfinkel, Harold, 1956. Conditions of successful degradation ceremonies. *American Journal of Sociology, 61,* 420-24.

Goffman, Erving, 1959. *The presentation of self in everyday life.* Garden City, N.Y.: Doubleday and Company.

Greenfield, Sidney M., 1961. Industrialization and the family in sociological theory. *American Journal of Sociology, 67,* 312-22.

Hempel, Carl, 1959. The logic of functionalism. In Llewellyn Gross (ed.), *Symposium on sociological theory.* Evanston, Ill.: Row, Peterson and Company.

Homans, George C., 1941. Anxiety and ritual: the theories of Malinowski and Radcliffe-Brown. *American Anthropologist, 43,* 164-72.

——, 1951. *The human group.* London: Routledge and Kegan Paul.

Hyman, Herbert, 1955. *Survey design and analysis.* Glencoe, Ill.: Free Press.

Jenks, A. E., 1905. *The Bontoc Igorot.* Manila: Bureau of Public Printing.

Kardiner, Abram, 1939. *The individual and his society.* New York: Columbia University Press. With a foreword and two ethnological reports by R. Linton.

Klapp, Orrin E., 1962. *Heroes, villains and fools.* Englewood Cliffs, N.J.: Prentice-Hall.

Lambert, William W., and Wallace E. Lambert, 1964. *Social psychology.* Englewood Cliffs, N.J.: Prentice-Hall.

Lazarsfeld, Paul F., 1955. Interpretation of statistical relations as a research operation. In P. F. Lazarsfeld and Morris Rosenberg, *The language of social research.* Glencoe, Ill.: Free Press.

Linton, Ralph, 1943. Nativistic movements. *American Anthropologist, 45,* 230-40.

——, 1956. *Culture and mental disorders.* Springfield, Ill.: Charles C. Thomas.

McClelland, David C., 1961. *The achieving society*. Princeton, N.J.: D Van Nostrand.

Mead, Margaret, 1959. *Growing up in New Guinea*. New York: New American Library.

——, 1961. *New lives for old*. New York: New American Library.

Menzel, Herbert, 1953. A new coefficient for scalogram analysis. *Publi Opinion Quarterly, 17,* 268-81.

Merton, R. K., 1957. Manifest and latent functions. In his *Social theor; and social structure,* rev. ed. Glencoe, Ill.: Free Press.

Miller, Nathan, 1932. Initiation. *Encyclopaedia of the social sciences*. New York: Macmillan. Vol. 8, pp. 49-50.

Munroe, Robert L., 1959. Couvade. Mimeographed interdisciplinary paper, Harvard University, Department of Social Relations.

Murdock, G. P., 1949. *Social structure*. New York: Macmillan.

——, 1957. World ethnographic sample. *American Anthropologist, 59* 664-87.

——, 1961. The cross-cultural survey. In Frank W. Moore, (ed.), *Read ings in cross-cultural methodology*. New Haven: Human Relation. Area Files.

Murphy, Robert F., 1959. Social structure and sex antagonism. *South western Journal of Anthropology, 15,* 89-98.

Nagel, E., 1956. A formalization of functionalism. In his *Logic withou metaphysics*. Glencoe, Ill.: Free Press.

Naroll, Raoul, 1961. Two solutions to Galton's problem. In Frank W Moore (ed.), *Readings in cross-cultural methodology*. New Haven Human Relations Area Files.

Norbeck, Edward, 1961. *Religion in primitive society*. New York: Harpe and Brothers.

Radcliffe-Brown, A. R., 1948. *The Andaman Islanders*. Glencoe, Ill.: Fre Press.

——, 1956. *Structure and function in primitive society*. Glencoe, Ill.: Fre Press.

Redfield, Robert, 1941. *The folk culture of Yucatan*. Chicago: University of Chicago Press.

——, 1947. The folk society. *American Journal of Sociology, 52,* 293-308

——, 1956. *Peasant society and culture*. Chicago: University of Chicag Press.

Selvin, Hanan C., 1957. A critique of tests of significance in survey researck *American Sociological Review, 22,* 519-27.

Service, Elman R., 1955. Indian-European relations in colonial Latir America. *American Anthropologist, 57,* 411-25.

Steward, Julian, 1955. *Theory of culture change*. Urbana, Ill.: University of Illinois Press.

Swanson, Guy E., 1960. *The birth of the gods*. Ann Arbor: University of Michigan Press.

Tylor, Edward, 1961. On a method of investigating the development of institutions. In Frank W. Moore (ed.), *Readings in cross-cultural methodology*. New Haven: Human Relations Area Files.

Valentine, C. A., 1961. *Masks and men in a Melanesian society*. Lawrence, Kansas: University of Kansas Publications.

Van Gennep, Arnold, 1960. *The rites of passage*. Tr. Monika B. Vizedom and Gabrielle L. Caffee. Chicago: University of Chicago Press.

Wallace, Anthony F. C., 1956. Revitalization movements. *American Anthropologist, 58,* 264-81.

——, 1961 a. *Culture and personality*. New York: Random House.

——, 1961 b. The psychic unity of human groups. In Bert Kaplan (ed.), *Studying personality cross-culturally*. Evanston, Ill.: Row, Peterson and Company.

Warner, W. Lloyd, 1958. *A black civilization*, rev. ed. New York: Harper and Brothers.

Webster, Hutton, 1938. *Primitive secret societies*. New York: Macmillan.

Whiting, John W. M., 1954. The cross-cultural method. In Gardner Lindzey (ed.), *Handbook of social psychology*. Cambridge, Mass.: Addison-Wesley Company.

——, 1961. Socialization process and personality. In Francis L. K. Hsu (ed.), *Psychological anthropology*. Homewood, Ill.: Dorsey Press.

——, 1962. Comment. *American Journal of Sociology, 67,* 391-94.

Whiting, J. W. M., and I. L. Child, 1953. *Child training and personality*. New Haven: Yale University Press.

Whiting, J. W. M., Richard Kluckhohn, and Albert Anthony, 1958. The function of male initiation ceremonies at puberty. In E. E. Maccoby, T. M. Newcomb, and E. L. Hartley (eds.), *Readings in social psychology*. New York: Henry Holt and Company. Pp. 359-70.

Young, Frank W., 1962. The function of male initiation ceremonies: a cross-cultural test of an alternative hypothesis. *American Journal of Sociology, 67,* 379-96.

Young, Frank W., and Ruth C. Young, 1962. The sequence and direction of community growth: a cross-cultural generalization. *Rural Sociology, 27,* 374-86.

Zelditch, Morris, 1959. *A basic course in sociological statistics*. New York: Henry Holt and Company.

Sources for the Study Sample

ALORESE (Atimelang, 1938)

DuBois, Cora, 1944. *The people of Alor.* Minneapolis: University o Minnesota Press.

Kardiner, A., *et al.*, 1945. *The psychological frontiers of society.* Nev York: Columbia University Press. Pp. 101-258.

ARAUCANIANS (Cautinche, 1948)

Titiev, Mischa, 1951. *Araucanian culture in transition.* Ann Arbor University of Michigan Museum of Anthropology.

ASHANTI (peasants, 1920)

Fortes, Meyer, 1950. Kinship and marriage among the Ashanti. I A. R. Radcliffe-Brown and Daryll Forde (eds.), *African systems c kinship and marriage.* London: Oxford University Press. Pp. 252-84.

Rattray, R. S., 1927. *Religion and art in Ashanti.* Oxford: Clarendor Press.

———, 1929. *Ashanti law and constitution.* Oxford: Clarendon Press.

AZANDE (1920)

Evans-Pritchard, E. E., 1937. *Witchcraft, oracles and magic amon; the Azande.* Oxford: Clarendon Press.

Larken, P. M., 1926-27. An account of the Zande. *Sudan Notes an, Records, 9,* 1-55; *10,* 85-134.

Seligman, C. G., and Brenda Seligman, 1932. The Azande. In thei *Pagan tribes of the Nilotic Sudan.* London: George Routledge and Sons Pp. 495-539.

BALINESE (Belaluan, 1930)

Covarrubias, Miguel, 1938. *Island of Bali.* New York: Alfred Knopf

BONTOC IGOROT (Bontoc, 1903)

Jenks, A. E., 1905. *The Bontoc Igorot.* Manila: Bureau of Publi Printing.

CAGABA (1947)
Reichel-Dolmatoff, Gerado, 1950. Los Kogi. *Revista del Instituto Etnológico Nacional,* No. 4, 2 vols. Bogota: Colombia Editorial Iqueima.

CAMAYURA (Juatuare, 1948)
Oberg, Kalervo, 1953. *Indian tribes of northern Mato Grosso, Brazil.* Washington: Smithsonian Institution, Institute of Social Anthropology, No. 15.

CHAGGA (Machame area, 1910)
Dundas, Charles, 1924. *Kilimanjaro and its people.* London: Witherby.
Raum, O. F., 1940. *Chagga childhood: a description of indigenous education in an East African tribe.* London: Oxford University Press.

CHEYENNE (northern, 1850)
Grinnell, G. B., 1923. *The Cheyenne Indians, their history and ways of life,* 2 vols. New Haven: Yale University Press.

CHIRICAHUA (1870)
Opler, Morris E., 1941. *An Apache life-way.* Chicago: University of Chicago Press.

DAHOMEANS (Abomey, 1931)
Herskovits, M. J., 1938. *Dahomey, an ancient West Africa kingdom,* 2 vols. New York: J. J. Augustin.

EGYPTIANS (Silwa, 1951)
Ammar, Hamed, 1954. *Growing up in an Egyptian village.* London: Routledge and Kegan Paul.

ESKIMOS (Copper Eskimos around Coronation Gulf, 1914)
Jenness, D., 1922. The life of the Copper Eskimo. *Report of the Canadian Arctic Expedition, 12* (1913-18). Ottawa: Acland.

FIJIANS (Tokalau, 1934)
Thompson, Laura, 1940a. *Southern Lau, Fiji; an ethnography.* Honolulu: Bernice P. Bishop Museum, Bulletin 162.
———, 1940b. *Fijian frontier.* San Francisco: Institute of Pacific Research.

FRENCH (Peyrane, 1950)
Wylie, L., 1957. *Village in the Vaucluse.* Cambridge, Mass.: Harvard University Press.

GANDA (peasants, 1900)
Roscoe, J., 1911. *The Baganda.* London: Macmillan.

HOPI (Hotavila, 1938)
Dennis, W., 1940. *The Hopi child*. New York: Appleton-Century.

JAPANESE (Suye Mura, 1936)
Embree, John F., 1939. *Suye Mura, a Japanese village*. Chicago: University of Chicago Press.

JIVARO (Achuare group, 1922)
Karsten, Rafael, 1935. *The head-hunters of western Amazonas*. Helsingfors: Centraltryckeriet.
Stirling, Matthew Williams, 1938. *History and ethnographical material on the Jivaro Indians*. Washington: Smithsonian Institution, Bureau of American Ethnology, Bulletin 117.

KORYAK (maritime, 1900)
Jochelson, W., 1905-08. The Koryak. *Memoirs of the American Museum of Natural History*, No. 19.

KWAKIUTL (Fort Rupert, 1900)
Benedict, Ruth, 1946. *Patterns of culture*. New York: Penguin Books.
Boas, Franz, 1895. *The social organization and secret societies of the Kwakiutl*. U.S. National Museum Report.
Ford, Clellan, 1941. *Smoke from their fires*. New Haven: Yale University Press.

KWOMA (Rumbima, 1936)
Whiting, J. W. M., 1941. *Becoming a Kwoma*. New Haven: Yale University Press.

LAKHERS (especially Savang, 1926)
Parry, N. E., 1932. *The Lakhers*. London: Macmillan.

LAMBA (Mushili district, 1917)
Doke, Clement M., 1931. *The Lambas of Northern Rhodesia*. London: G. G. Harrap.

LAPPS (nomadic in Sweden, 1875)
The Lapps. Indiana University, Subcontractor's Monograph, HRAF-3, Indiana-6, prepared for the Human Relations Area Files, 1955.
Turi, J., 1931. *Turi's book of Lappland*. London: Cape.

LEPCHAS (Lingtem, 1937)
Gorer, G., 1938. *Himalayan village*. London: Michael Joseph.
Morris, J., 1938. *Living with Lepchas*. London: William Heinemann.

MALAITA (bush group, 1933)
Hogbin, H. Ian, 1939. *Experiment in civilization*. London: George Routledge and Sons.

MAORI (North Island, 1850)
Best, E., 1924. *The Maori*. Wellington: Tombs.
Markerti, 1938. *The old time Maori*. Ed. T. K. Penniman. London: Victor Gollancz.

MEXICANS (Tepoztlán, 1945)
Lewis, Oscar, 1951. *Life in a Mexican village: Tepoztlán restudied*. Urbana: University of Illinois Press.

MIXTEC (Santo Domingo, 1955)
Romney, A. K., personal communication.

NAVAHO (1943)
Kluckhohn, C., and D. Leighton, 1946. *The Navaho*. Cambridge, Mass.: Harvard University Press.
Leighton, D., and C. Kluckhohn, 1947. *Children of the people*. Cambridge, Mass.: Harvard University Press.

NEW IRELAND (Lesu, 1930)
Powdermaker, Hortense, 1933. *Life in Lesu*. New York: W. W. Norton.

NUER (1928)
Butt, Audrey, 1952. The Nilotes of the Anglo-Egyptian Sudan and Uganda. In Daryll Forde (ed.), *Ethnographic survey of Africa*. London: International African Institute. Pt. IV.
Evans-Pritchard, E. E., 1936. The Nuer: age sets. *Sudan Notes and Records, 19*, Pt. II.
———, 1940. *The Nuer: a description of the modes of livelihood and political institutions of a Nilotic people*. Oxford: Clarendon Press.
———, 1945. *Some aspects of marriage and the family among the Nuer*. Rhodes-Livingston Papers No. 11. Livingston, N. Rhodesia: Rhodes-Livingston Institute.
———, 1951. *Kinship and marriage among the Nuer*. Oxford: Clarendon Press.
Huffman, Ray, 1931. *Nuer customs and folk-lore*. London: Oxford University Press.

NYAKYUSA (Nu Ngonde, 1936)
Wilson, Monica, 1952. *Good company, a study of Nyakyusa age-villages*. London: Oxford University Press.

——, 1957. *Rituals of kinship among the Nyakyusa.* London: Oxford University Press.

——, 1959. *Communal rituals of the Nyakyusa.* New York: Oxford University Press.

OJIBWA (1850)

Densmore, Francis, 1929. *Chippewa customs.* Washington: Bureau of American Ethnology, Bulletin 86.

Hilger, M. Inez, 1951. *Chippewa child life and its cultural background.* Washington: Bureau of American Ethnology, Bulletin 146.

ONTONG JAVANESE (Luaniua and Pelau, 1928)

Hogbin, H. Ian, 1931. Education at Ontong Java, Solomon Islands. *American Anthropologist, 33,* 601-14.

——, 1931. The sexual life of the natives of Ontong-Java. *Journal of the Polynesian Society, 40,* 23-24.

——, 1931. The social organization of Ontong-Java. *Oceania, 1,* No. 4, 399-425.

——, 1931. Tribal ceremonies at Ontong-Java, Solomon Islands. *Journal of the Royal Anthropological Institute, 62,* 27-55.

——, 1934. *Law and order in Polynesia.* New York: Harcourt, Brace.

OOLDEA (1941)

Berndt, Ronald, and Catherine Berndt, 1942, 1943. A preliminary report of field work in the Ooldea Region, Western South Australia. *Oceania, 13,* 51-70, 143-69, 243-80, 362-75; *14,* 30-66, 124-58, 220-49, 338-58.

PAPAGO (Hichwian and Gu Vo, 1942)

Joseph, Alice, Rosamond Spicer, and Jane Chesky, 1949. *The desert people.* Chicago: University of Chicago Press.

PILAGA (1936)

Henry, Jules. Personal communication.

——, 1940. Some cultural determinants of hostility in Pilaga Indian children. *American Journal of Orthopsychiatry, 10,* No. 1, 111-22.

Henry, J., and Z. Henry, 1944. *Doll-play of Pilaga Indian children.* New York: Orthopsychiatric Association, Monograph Series, No. 4.

PONDO (Tibane, 1933)

Hunter, Monica, 1936. *Reaction to conquest: effects of contact with Europeans on the Pondo of South Africa.* London: Oxford University Press.

SAMOANS (middle class in Manua, 1926)
Mead, Margaret, 1930. *Social Organization of Manua.* Honolulu: Bernice P. Bishop Museum, Bulletin 76.

SERBS (Orasac, 1953)
Halpern, Joel M., 1958. *A Serbian village.* New York: Columbia University Press.

SIRIONO (1940)
Holmberg, Allan R., 1950. *Nomads of the Long Bow.* Smithsonian Museum Publications in Social Anthropology, No. 10. Washington, D.C.: U.S. Government Printing Office.

TALLENSI (rural, 1934)
Fortes, Meyer, 1945. *Dynamics of clanship among the Tallensi.* London: Oxford University Press.
———, 1949. *The web of kinship among the Tallensi.* London: Oxford University Press.

TANALA (Menabe, 1926)
Linton, R., 1933. The Tanala. *Anthropological Survey Field Museum of Natural History, 22.*
———, 1939. The Tanala of Madagascar. In A. Kardiner, *The individual and his society.* New York: Columbia University Press. Pp. 251-90.

THONGA (northern clans, 1910)
Junod, Henri A., 1927. *The life of a South African tribe,* 2 vols., 2nd rev. ed. London: Macmillan.

TIMBIRA (Ramcocamecra, 1932)
Nimuendaju, Curt, 1946. The Eastern Timbira. Tr. and ed. Robert H. Lowie. *University of California Publications in American Archeology and Ethnology,* No. 41.

TIV (1920)
Bohanan, Paul, and Laura Bohanan. *The Tiv of Central Nigeria.* London: International African Institute.
East, Rupert (ed.) 1939. *Akiga's story: the Tiv tribe as seen by one of its members.* London: Oxford University Press.

TROBRIANDERS (Omarakana, 1917)
Malinowski, B., 1927. *Sex and repression in savage society.* New York: Harcourt, Brace.
———, 1929. *The sexual life of savages.* New York: Horace Liveright.

TRUKESE (1947)

Gladwin, Thomas, and Seymour Sarason, 1953. Truk: man in paradise. *Viking Fund Publications in Anthropology*, No. 20.

Goodenough, W. H., 1951. Property, kin and community on Truk. *Yale University Publications in Anthropology*, No. 46.

UNITED STATES (Homestead, 1950)

Vogt, E. Z., 1955. *Modern homesteaders.* Cambridge, Mass.: Belnap Press of Harvard University Press.

YAGUA (1940)

Fejos, Paul, 1943. Ethnography of the Yagua. *Viking Fund Publications in Anthropology*, No. 1.

YAP (Fal, 1948)

Schneider, David. Personal Communication.

——, 1949. The kinship system and village organization of Yap. Doctoral thesis, Harvard University.

——, 1953. Yap kinship terminology and kin groups. *American Anthropologist*, 55, 215-36.

Sources for the Auxiliary Sample

ANDAMANS (northern coastal group, 1850)
Radcliffe-Brown, A. R., 1948. *The Andaman Islanders*. Glencoe, Ill.: Free Press.

ARANDA (Alice Springs, 1896)
Spencer, Baldwin, and F. J. Gillen, 1927. *The Arunta*. London: Macmillan.

AZANDE (1920)
Evans-Pritchard, E. E., 1937. *Witchcraft, oracles and magic among the Azande*. Oxford: Clarendon Press.
Larken, P. M., 1926-27. An account of the Zande. *Sudan Notes and Records*, 9, 1-55; 10, 85-134.
Seligman, C. G., and Brenda Seligman, 1932. The Azande. In their *Pagan tribes of the Nilotic Sudan*. London: George Routledge and Sons. Pp. 495-539.

CALLINAGO (Island of Guadeloupe, 1650-1700)
Breton, Raymond, 1665. *Caribe-French dictionary*. Tr. Marshall McKusick and P. Verin. Auxerre: Gilles Bouquet.
Breton, R., and Armand de la Paix, 1929. An account of the island of Guadeloupe. *Histoire Coloniale*, *I*, 45-74. Paris: Librairie Générale et Internationale. Trans. for *HRAF* by Thomas Turner.
Rouse, I., 1948. The Carib. In Julian Steward (ed.), *Handbook of South American Indians*. Washington: U.S. Government Printing Office.

COMANCHE (1800)
Wallace, Ernest, and E. A. Hoebel, 1952. *The Comanches: lords of the south plains*. Norman: University of Oklahoma Press.

ILA (Mala, 1940)
Tuden, Arthur. Personal communication based on field work in 1956-58.

KATAB (1931)

Gunn, Harold D., 1956. Pagan peoples of the central area of Northern Nigeria. In Daryll Forde (ed.), *Ethnographic survey of Africa, Western Africa*, Pt. XII. London: International African Institute.

Meek, C. K., 1931. *Tribal studies in Northern Nigeria*. London: Kegan Paul, Trench, Trubner and Co., II, 1-128.

LOVEDU (1936-38)

Krige, E. J., and J. D. Krige, 1947. *The realm of the rain queen*. New York: Oxford University Press.

LUO (1925)

Butt, A., 1952. The Nilotes of the Anglo-Egyptian Sudan and Uganda. In Daryll Forde (ed.), *Ethnographic survey of Africa*. London: International African Institute. Pt. IV.

MALEKULA (Vao, 1914)

Lagard, John, 1942. *Stone men of Malekula*. London: Chatto & Windus.

MANDAN (Like-a-Fishook, 1870)

Bowers, A. W., 1950. *Mandan social and ceremonial organization*. Chicago: University of Chicago Press.

MARQUESANS (1842)

Handy, E. S., 1923. *The native culture in the Marquesas*. Honolulu: Bernice P. Bishop Museum, Bulletin 9.

Linton, Ralph, 1939. Marquesan Culture. In Kardiner, A., *The individual and his society*. New York: Columbia University Press. Pp. 137-96.

MOSSI (Gurcy, 1956)

Hammond, Peter. Personal communications based on field work in 1956.

NEW IRELAND (Lesu, 1930)

Powdermaker, Hortense, 1933. *Life in Lesu*. New York: W. W. Norton.

OJIBWA (1850)

Densmore, Francis, 1929. *Chippewa customs*. Washington: Bureau of American Ethnology, Bulletin 86.

Hilger, M. Inez, 1951. *Chippewa child life and its cultural background*. Washington: Bureau of American Ethnology, Bulletin 146.

SHILLUK (1932)

Butt, A., 1952. The Nilotes of the Anglo-Egyptian Sudan and Uganda. In Daryll Forde (ed.), *Ethnographic survey of Africa*. London: International African Institute. Pt. IV.

Howell, P. P., 1941. The Shilluk settlement. *Sudan Notes and Records*, *24*, 47-68.

Pumphrey, M. E. C., 1941. The Shilluk tribe. *Sudan Notes and Records*, *24*, 1-45.

Seligman, C. G., and Brenda Seligman, 1932. *Pagan tribes of the Nilotic Sudan*. London: George Routledge & Sons. Pp. 37-105.

Westermann, Diedrich, 1912. *The Shilluk people: their language and folklore*. Philadelphia: Board of Foreign Missions of the United Presbyterian Church of North America.

SOUTHEAST SALISH (Sinkaietk, 1850)

Cline, W., R. S. Commons, M. Mandelbaum, R. H. Post, and L. V. W. Walters, 1938. *The Sinkaietk on the Southern Okanagon of Washington*. Ed. L. Spier. Menasha, Wis.: George Banta.

TAPIRAPE (Tampitawa, 1939)

Wagley, C., and Eduardo Galvao. The Tapirape. In Julian Steward (ed.), *Handbook of South American Indians*, *3*, 167-78.

TASMANIANS (1800)

Roth, H. L., 1896. *The aborigines of Tasmania*. London: Kegan Paul, Trench, Trubner and Co.

TIKOPIA (Matautu, 1928-29)

Firth, R., 1936. *We, the Tikopia*. New York: American Book Company.

Rivers, W. H. R., 1914. *The history of Melanesian society*. Cambridge: Cambridge University Press. I, Ch. 12.

TIMBIRA (Ramcocamecra, 1932)

Nimeundaju, Curt, 1941. The Eastern Timbira. Tr. and ed. Robert H. Lowie. *University of California Publications in American Archeology and Ethnology*, No. 41.

TIV (1920)

East, Rupert, (ed.) 1939. *Akiga's story: the Tiv tribe as seen by one of its members*. London: Oxford University Press.

Bohanan, Paul, and Laura Bohanan, 1953. *The Tiv of Central Nigeria*. London: International African Institute.

WOLOF (rural Sengambia, probably village of Njau, 1948)

Aimes, David W., 1958. Plural marriage among the Wolof in Gambia. Northwestern University, doctoral dissertation.

——, 1959. Wolof co-operative work groups. In W. R. Bascom and M. J. Herskovits (eds.), *Continuity and change in African cultures*. Chicago: University of Chicago Press.

Gamble, David D., 1957. The Wolof of Sengambia. In Daryll Forde (ed.), *Ethnographic survey of Africa*. London: International African Institute.

Gorer, Geoffrey, 1935. *Africa dances*. London: Faber and Faber.

YOKUTS (Central Foothills, 1850)

Gayton, A. H., 1948. Yokuts and Western Mono ethnography. I: Tulare Lake, Southern Valley and Central Foothills. *University of California Publications in Anthropological Records, 10*, 1-142.

ZUNI (1890)

Eggan, Fred, 1950. *Social organization of the Western Pueblos*. Chicago: University of Chicago Press. Pp. 176-222.

Kroeber, A. L., 1917. Zuni kin and clan. *Anthropological papers of the American Museum of Natural History, 18*, Pt. 3,

Parsons, Elsie C., 1917. Zuni conception and pregnancy beliefs. *Proceedings of the 19th International Congress of Americanists*, 379-83.

——, 1919. Mothers and children of Zuni, New Mexico. *Man, 19*, 168-73.

Stevenson, Matilda Core, 1901-02. The Zuni Indians: their mythology, esoteric societies and ceremonies. *Twenty-third Annual Report of the Bureau of American Ethnology*. Pp. 1-634.

Index

Aberle, D. F., 147, 148-149
  quoted, 148*n*.
acculturation (*see* community-nation articulation; social change)
achievement motivation, 33, 159, 161, 162, 163-164
adolescence (*see* initiation ceremonies, female; initiation ceremonies, male; puberty)
age
  as criterion in initiation ceremonies, 12, 13
  social recognition of levels of, 11
age grades, 65, 66
agriculture
  modern, 87-95, 99, 127
  traditional, 87-95, 99-100
  (*see also* horticulture)
American society, 114, 117, 125, 133, 136, 137
Americans (Homestead Texans), 43, 90, 98
Anthony, Albert, 5
  quoted, 42-43
Apache, 12, 124
Araucanians, 98
Aronson, Elliot, 79-80
  quoted, 79-80
articulation (*see* community-nation articulation)
audience
  of initiation ceremonies, 11, 16, 22, 73-74

audience—*Cont.*
  role of, in dramatization concept, 3, 25-26, 63, 150
Australian aborigines, 12, 29*n*. (*see also* Ooldea)
Azande, 74, 76

Bales, R. F., 139, 145
Balinese, 71, 102, 124
beatings (*see* hazings)
Benedict, Ruth, quoted, 25
Bettelheim, Bruno, 4
birth customs (*see* parenthood ceremonies)
Blake, Judith, 118*n*.
Boas, Franz, 102
Bontoc Igorot, 74, 75, 82, 83
Burke, Kenneth, 3, 150, 154

Cagaba, 71
Camayura, 116, 124
Cancian, Francesca, 27*n*., 145
  quoted, 145
Chagga, 68, 124
change (*see* community-national articulation; social change)
Chapple, E. D., 38, 39
  quoted, 38
Charles, Lucille H., quoted, 9
Cheyenne, 105, 123
childhood, rituals of, 81, 82, 83
child-rearing practices, 33, 34, 35, 46, 136-137, 159, 163

193